Collecting Books for Fun and Profit

Collecting Books for Fun and Profit

Arthur H. Minters

ARCO PUBLISHING, INC.
219 PARK AVENUE SOUTH, NEW YORK, N.Y. 10003

Published by Arco Publishing, Inc.
219 Park Avenue South, New York, N.Y. 10003

Copyright © 1979 by Arthur H. Minters

Library of Congress Cataloging in Publication Data

Minters, Arthur H
   Collecting books for fun and profit.

   Bibliography: p. 151
   Includes index.
   1. Book collecting.   I. Title.
Z987.M55   020'.75   79-10501
ISBN 0-668-04598-1

Printed in the United States of America

Acknowledgments

This book owes its existence to my wife, Frances, who nagged the life out of me until I wrote it, and who gave me professional editorial advice. Without her, this book would still be all talk.

There are so many other people who deserve thanks that it's impossible to list all of them, so I'll just say thanks to Kay, for her help in the starting years, and to some of the "hungries" who were always so eager for good material: Frank Hanlin, bibliographer of the University of Iowa libraries; Jens Nyholm, former director of libraries at Northwestern University; Richard Press, former collection development librarian at Northwestern; Hunter Adams, former architecture librarian at the University of Kentucky; Berna Neal, architecture librarian at the University of Maryland; Kerry Zack, former art librarian at Indiana University; Jim Humphry III, former art librarian at the Metropolitan Museum of Art; and Anne Wozar, order librarian at the Metropolitan. To the late E. Seligmann, a dealer's dealer, and to Carl Simonsen, for his love of ephemera. And to my daughters, Elizabeth and Michèle, who begged me to stop telling them about my experiences, and to bug someone else instead.

For the photographs, I thank photographer Michael Abramson; Dr. Stanley T. Lewis; Christie, Manson & Woods International, Inc., especially Stephen C. Massey, director, rare books and manuscripts, and David B. Ryan, photographer; and Showcraft International, Inc., and its president, Stanley M. Finn.

Finally, my thanks to all the artists, scribes, printers, typesetters, and papermakers whose efforts through the ages have made the art of the book what it is today.

Preface

For too long there has been an unconscious elitist ambiance surrounding book collecting. I for one would like to see the trend reversed or altogether dispelled. You don't need a lot of money, or a college education, or extensive previous preparation, to love books and want to collect them.

Think of the immigrants who came to this country penniless, who after a hard day at manual work would go to the opera and stand through the performance. They did not feel they had to justify their attendance; opera turned them on, so they went.

In the same way, if books turn you on—even if the attraction is, as yet, dormant—let yourself enjoy them. Collecting books can be a means of self-discovery, an exciting way to find the unknown you. All it takes is for you to sit back and allow your feelings to surface and speak to you, to remind you of past times when you were excited, to recall what you were excited about. Then you can retrace these experiences and put them in the present, and this time act on them. It is easier than you imagine.

When we start out in a new endeavor, we need a guide to show us the way. I hope that this book will provide you with that guide. It isn't going to tell you which are the most important books to collect—that's up to you to decide—or which edition of Shakespeare is the best. What it is going to do is to give you the confidence in your own self, in your own tastes and judgment, to go on and find out for yourself which subjects, authors, and areas really interest you, move you, stimulate you to gather more and more of them onto a shelf until you see or feel that you are truly a collector.

This book will explain the methodology of selecting, ordering, paying for, cataloguing, and caring for your collection. It will outline the cycle of buying and maintaining the collection and eventually of disposing of those parts of it that no longer fit your needs. Once procedures have been established, the whole cycle should flow in an orderly fashion, and you should find satisfaction in each part of it.

My hope is not only that you enjoy my book, but that it will provide you with the means of getting more enjoyment from other books as well.

Happy collecting!

Contents

Illustrations

at the Plaza Hotel, April 1978, and there I am, walking toward the camera. *Photo by Showcraft International, Inc.*

PLATE 7. A slipcase that is enclosed on all but one side creates a partial vacuum, causing the book to stick when removed, and eventually destroying the backstrip. *Photo by Michael Abramson.*

PLATE 8. The clam shell box, which has an attached cover, is the best type of box for books and periodicals. *Photo by Michael Abramson.*

PLATE 9. A glass-fronted bookcase provides maximum protection for books. *Photo by Michael Abramson.*

PLATE 10. This volume was kept on the lowest shelf of an open bookcase; notice the mop splatters on the cover. *Photo by Michael Abramson.*

Collecting Books
for Fun and Profit

CHAPTER 1

Why Collect Books?

Many people ask me that question. "Why should I collect books when I can borrow them from the library or from friends or relatives?" And my answer is always the same. If you borrow books, you have to return them someday, and thus the bond between you and the book is never established. It is this bond that I feel is really important—the relationship between the owner and the book. A borrowed book isn't yours, and you can't do the things with it that you could do if you owned it. You can't put it away in a special place, or look at it whenever you like, or consult it for reference or pleasure. You can't feel free with it, since the volume is on loan and you have the responsibility of taking care of it until it is returned to the owner or library.

Borrowing is fine for books that you want to skim through once, but not for collecting. There is a special commitment that is inherent in collecting books and printed matter. In many respects it is the same commitment that should be present when one is in love: a strong desire to be with the person, to care for the person, to hold the person because he or she is beautiful, to give of yourself as well as to be open to the one you love, to share your world with others, and to be together as long as you both have these feelings. A casual acquaintance cannot provide all of these ingredients in a permanent way, nor can a borrowed book.

There is something in the human condition that is attracted to beauty and mystery. Books have both. Like a plant, books have to be nurtured. They have to be planted in the soil of possession; otherwise they are like cut flowers, which are beautiful when they are fresh, but wilt and die in a matter of days. Of course, there are occasions when we want the bookish equivalent of cut flowers—and on such occasions, borrowing and libraries fit the temporary need.

THE ANCIENT ART OF BOOK COLLECTING

Scribes and artists have been respected throughout history, and so has the collecting of their works. You don't have to be an archaeologist or an anthropologist to collect the signs and symbols of a given culture, nor is it necessary to become an explorer in far-off lands. The only exploring needed is to look within yourself and discover what it is you would like to find. Let this book be your compass in this discovery. . . .

As far back as the Stone Age, when caves such as the ones discovered in Altamira were decorated with images, artists and their assistants were given special status and privileges. These decorators were exempt from battle and other manual work and were given the best food, clothes, and lodgings. They were held in high esteem by their communities. The images that they depicted were seen by the entire tribe. Pictures of the hunt and of tributes to deities were on the walls for all to marvel at and to partake in vicariously.

Later, as written language was developed, the duties of recording the tribe's achievements and invoking its gods passed from the artist to the scribe. The scribe occupied an important position in the court, in the kingdom, and, later, in the church. An Egyptian sculpture, "Seated Scribe," now in the Louvre, dates back to about 2500 B.C. It shows an impressively dignified official. It must have been a great honor to record the events of the pharaoh's court.

Many ancient writings were carefully preserved, because they were sacred, because they told of the society's history, or simply because they were good stories that people liked to read or listen to. The Babylonians, Assyrians, and Egyptians all had libraries. Under Greek influence, the libraries at Alexandria became the most celebrated in the ancient world. In Rome, emperors from the time of Augustus Caesar on established public libraries, and private collecting was a fashion indulged in by many Romans, including Cicero and Atticus.

But perhaps the art of book collecting really came into its own during the Renaissance. It was then that the literary contributions of antiquity—the Hebrew, Greek, and Latin manuscripts that had been preserved in the libraries of the monasteries during the relatively unlettered Middle Ages—were rediscovered by artists and patrons of the arts. In Italy, particularly, these literary treasures came to be considered foundation stones of knowledge. Writers and artists drew their inspiration from them. The poet Petrarch owned and took exceptional care of his copy of a Greek manuscript of Homer's—which, by the way, he couldn't read.

In the fifteenth century more translations were made from the Greek, and collectors began to assemble libraries made up of original manuscripts or hand copies. It is to such collectors that we owe the preservation of the ancient literature. One collector was Pope Nicholas V, whose book buying put him in debt when he was still a monk. When he became pope, he employed what we would today call book scouts to search for books for him. Pope Nicholas left a collection of some 9,000 volumes, which formed the foundation of the Vatican library.

Another Renaissance figure who got into trouble buying books was Niccolò Niccoli of Florence. When his money ran out, the Medicis subsidized him. Niccoli's collection is now part of the Laurentian library. The Medicis' own collection is there as well.

While these and many similar literary adventures were taking place, the passion for collecting was criticized by people who worried that harm would come from this manic pursuit of books.

It seems that some collectors were willing to sacrifice all they possessed in order to buy books. So, you see, the madness is quite old. My own father used to go a little hungry in czarist Russia so that he could buy books, especially the Nick Carter series— which wasn't required reading for his courses at the gymnasium. At night, when he was supposed to be asleep, he was under his blanket reading Nick Carter with the aid of a lantern or flashlight. In the Bronx, I used to read in the bathroom when I was supposed to be asleep. An obsession with books is not uncommon and, in most cases, once we get hooked the disease is incurable.

THE BEGINNINGS OF PRINTING

In 1450 Johann Gutenberg of Mainz introduced printing with movable type. At first printing met with little enthusiasm from collectors. Accustomed to the beautiful calligraphy, fine parchment, and elegant bindings of Renaissance manuscripts, they regarded printed books with the same scorn many collectors today have for paperbacks. Duke Federigo of Urbino, whose library is now in the Vatican, is reported to have said that he would be ashamed to own a printed book. But for the students, lawyers, and others who could not afford to hire copyists and had thus been forced to copy their reading materials themselves by hand, printed books were sheer pleasure.

Actually, the Chinese had invented printing, using a woodblock and paper, as far back as 594 A.D. The process gradually spread along the caravan routes to the West. Block books and block prints were printed before Gutenberg, but a woodblock deteriorates after some copies. Gutenberg used metal type, and also individual letters instead of blocks. Thus it became possible to edit or correct the work carefully, and to mass market identical copies of a text. Along with his marvelous books, Gutenberg also printed ephemera—pamphlets, calendars, and indulgences—thus becoming the first job printer. He also invented the means of reproducing the metal letters by moulds, and he invented a printer's ink. His kind of press remained in use without really any substantial changes or improvements for more than three centuries.

Gutenberg died in 1468. By 1485 printing presses had been installed throughout western Europe, and printing was in full swing. While the earliest printers closely followed the design and script of the contemporary manuscripts, even down to the hand-colored illustrations or illuminated initials, by 1480 printers had begun changing the appearance of the printed page and beginning what we now take for granted as the authentic book look. Early on, Roman type was introduced as an alternative to the harder-to-read Gothic type favored by Gutenberg; in fact, the first book printed in Italy, Cicero's *De Oratore*, in 1465, was in Roman type. The design of new typefaces continues to this day.

The German printers who spread printing throughout Europe in the fifteenth and sixteenth centuries realized that there was a market for inexpensive books. They sold their books to people of moderate means, not to the aristocracy, who still looked down on the printed book. It is therefore ironic that today early printed books are priced way out of the reach of most collectors; in 1978 a Gutenberg Bible was sold to the Baden-Wurttemberg State Museum in Stuttgart for two million dollars, and other early printed books fetch prices almost as large. But for those of you who are interested in early printing and incunabula (books printed before 1501; the singular is incunabulum), the history of the development of paper, presses, and printing is an excellent subject for collecting.

MOTIVES FOR COLLECTING BOOKS

But why should you, in the twentieth century, collect books? There are probably as many reasons as there are book collectors. Some people simply love books—all books. Others want to possess books that are beautiful. Others want to collect all they can about a particular subject. Others are interested in the prestige or snob appeal of books (as valid a motive as any other). Others are interested in books as an investment. For others, the main appeal in book collecting lies in the thrill of the chase—the excitement of finding a rare book after a long search. Perhaps for most people a combination of several motives is involved.

Let's take a closer look at two important motives for collecting books: what I call the profit motive and the fun motive.

THE PROFIT MOTIVE

More and more collectors, banks, and investment houses are turning to books and other hard money items as an investment area, and rightfully so. On the average, a good out-of-print book appreciates at least 10 percent a year, and I have found that in my areas it is even higher. One has only to check the auction records, dealers' catalogues, and store prices for a confirmation of this fact. And, unlike the buyer of stocks or bonds, the book investor has the pleasure of reading the books while his or her investment appreciates.

Not every investor reads his books, however. I met a collector at a European auction who told me that he'd started investing in books in 1957 when he'd had some spare cash, 1,000 Swiss francs to be exact. What made this collector so unusual is that he never took physical possession of the books. Each year he bought books at auction and left them with the auctioneer to be auctioned off to other buyers the next year. Meanwhile, he used the anticipated profits to buy more books to resell the following year. He repeated this ritual with each successive auction. The inflationary spiral worked in his favor, and by the time I met him in 1969, his collection was worth approximately 100,000 Swiss francs.

Not everybody can duplicate this performance. The amount you can make by investing in books depends on the amount you invest, the material you invest in, and the time you are willing to wait for a return. A private collector usually cannot turn his or her books over immediately for a quick profit because, unlike stocks or bonds, books can't be sold through a broker. The market for books consists of booksellers, other collectors, libraries, and auction houses. It may take a year or even more to find a buyer for a collection. If the books are placed at auction, then you have to wait until the date of the sale (and then another couple of months until you get your check).

Within these limits, though, books are a great investment. I firmly believe that book prices will continue to rise as long as inflation continues. Paper money is worth less each year, and the simple supply and demand factors make hard goods such as books, paintings, and prints more valuable and more desirable as investment hedges. To take an example, in 1970 I was selling the periodical *Camera Work* for $40 to $50 a number. In 1978 these same numbers were selling for $2,000 to $3,500 per issue—quite a difference! Good photographic items in general are now in a tremendous boom; but the other items I sell are also almost impossible to replace at the prices I paid for them—I now have to pay as much or more to buy them as the prices I just sold them for.

So as long as we are in an inflationary spiral—and it looks as if this condition will be with us for some time to come—the demand for good out-of-print, scarce, and rare books will continue to grow as more and more collectors realize what a good investment books are. As with all supply and demand relationships, as the demand grows and the supply stands still—or even diminishes as the books vanish into libraries and private collections, or simply wear out—prices have no other place to go but up. So your investment will be secure as your collection grows. And meanwhile your pleasure in the books will grow, too.

THE FUN MOTIVE

Most of us aren't brought up to value the pursuit of happiness, although it is in our Declaration of Independence. So it is up to us to provide and ensure our own pleasures. Books, and collecting them, offer a pleasure that isn't easy to measure. But just stop and think about it. What other pursuit sharpens the eye, adds to our knowledge, provides us with a unique experience, and touches areas within us that haven't been accessible before?

There are a lot of fun things about book collecting—looking at, reading, touching the books, discussing them with other collectors—but to me one of the best things is the fun of finding a scarce book—the thrill of the chase. The search is really a quest to discover a part of one's unknown self, and there isn't anything as exciting as finding a book in a place where you least expect it to be.

When I think of the unexpected pleasures that I have had in my twenty years of book buying, the first place to come to mind is Madrid.

I never felt completely comfortable in Madrid during the Franco regime. I really went more to see the Prado and visit my favorite bookseller in the city, Libreria Mirto, than to buy books. One night, after a late dinner (early for Madrilenos), I was taking a long walk to help digest the six courses. Since I was off duty, so to speak—not looking for books—I was wandering without any fixed route.

I found myself in a section of town that I didn't recognize, where eighteenth-century buildings enclosed an impressive square. At the entrance to the square there was a large bronze medallion encased in the pavement, depicting Madrid as the center of the globe. The square itself was full of activity, flags flying, lots of people coming and going, and many police cars parked at one side; I later found out that secret police headquarters were there. Near the center of the square was a bookshop with a wired grate over the window. On a shelf in the window were several books, their spines turned to the street. As I walked past the shop, something caught my eye, and an alarm suddenly went off in my brain.

I sat down at a café, ordered a black coffee and a Carlos V brandy, lit up a Havana, and tried to shut off the alarm. So what if I had seen a red spine with a black diagonal. That didn't necessarily mean that the book was by a member of the constructivist school of art. Other people use diagonals, too. But on the other hand, if it were a constructivist design. . . . I slowly retraced my footsteps. I stood in front of the window, peering through the mesh grating at the red spine, which was sandwiched between typically Spanish bound quartos. There it was, stark and bare by comparison, neat, clean, and the black diagonal just right in proportion to the red cloth backstrip—just so damn modern, so constructivist, so un-*ungepatschkit*, that the bell went off again, and my nose began to itch. It could be by El Lissitzky, the leading Russian constructivist.

No, the rational mind said, impossible. A Lissitzky in Franco's Madrid? Strictly *verboten*—the police or the censors would have suppressed it (as they would have in the Soviet Union, too, by the way). Oh what pleasure, what irony, what justice—if only it were a Lissitzky, the antithesis of propagandist art, the best in modern design—what sweet revenge, my personal triumph against fascism. It all poured out, all my anti-fascist feelings, and all because of a red spine and a black diagonal.

I went back to the hotel trying to control myself, but it was no use. The gig was uncovered, and all I could think of was, was it or wasn't it a Lissitzky, and if it was, what the hell was it doing here? And I was going to buy it right under the noses of the authorities and take it with me—or, safer, mail it out. Oh, what joy, what pleasure! Realistically, I needed it for about nine customers, so if it was a Lissitzky it could be sold nine times over—but that was incidental. What was important was this constructivist survivor in the sea of Falangism.

I didn't fall asleep until 5 o'clock in the morning, and at 7:30 I was awakened by the desk clerk, as I had instructed. I wanted an early start. If the volume was a Lissitzky, I wasn't going to

let anyone else have it. I was going to get there first and buy it
regardless of the cost. I wanted to appear calm and cool, English
rather than emotional, but it was no use. I was too involved. I
had what I thought was the longest breakfast of my life and
started back to the square.

Things didn't look the same in the morning light. What if
I got lost and never found the place? The thought made me break
out in a cold sweat. Would some other foreigner buy it, or would
the police confiscate it before I arrived? The shop wouldn't open
until 10, but if I got lost. . . . But "the nose knows." I reached
the entrance to the square at exactly 9:03 and sat down at the
nearest café I could find. I was exhausted. I asked the waiter if
he knew the owner of the shop and would it open soon. He
answered that the owner would be there at 10. After I don't know
how many coffees, I spotted an elderly woman approaching the
shop. She pushed up the grate, opened the door, and slowly
stepped in.

I had settled my account earlier, so I was ready to go. But
remember, I told myself, you are in Spain, not on Fourth Avenue.
Be slow, polite, gracious, present your card, ask if there are any
books on art, architecture, modern literature—and then leap for
the window. *"Si, señor, mucho,"* she said, and took me to the back
of the shop, which was dark, uninteresting, and away from my
purpose in life. I slowly made my way to the front, stopping
several times to pull volumes from various places and return them
with a nod.

Finally I was at the window. I carefully removed the red volume.
I couldn't keep from smiling. It was Lissitzky's *Russland*, in
perfect condition, though not in its original binding—and I had
found it all by myself. Slowly I turned around and asked the
price. The woman said, "Two hundred pesetas." "Two hundred
pesetas!" I exclaimed. "Three dollars!" She was taken aback. "One
hundred and seventy pesetas," she bargained.

I paid her in cash, and, clutching the book to my chest, went back to my hotel to wrap it. Then I took a taxi to the central post office, where I sent it by registered air mail to the United States. That night I wrote my office that a treasure was on the way. When I got back home, I sent the book to the customer who had requested it first. The price at that time—this was in 1964—was $75; it goes for over $250 now. It was not a major find monetarily, but spiritually it was the best of the trip.

CHAPTER 2

Becoming a Collector

Probably you don't have to "become" a collector; actually, most of us *are* collectors, even if we don't know it. I am always amazed when I hear that a person has books and still doesn't acknowledge that what is physically present is at least the beginning of a collection. So the first thing to do is to tell yourself that *from now on you are a collector*. Keep this fact in your conscious mind. Believe me, that's all it takes to become a collector. It's as simple as that. You like books, you buy books, you keep them—and that is a collection.

If you don't have any books but you wish to start acquiring them, then you are a collector but haven't yet allowed yourself the pleasure of buying. Just say to yourself, "I deserve it," and go out and buy yourself a book. After you break the ice, you'll feel a lot better about buying other books.

Remember, you are a mature adult. You are in command of your own spending, and you can stay within a budget that you will control and that will take into account the space you have and the amount of books you wish to start with. You haven't got a place to keep your books? Buy a bookcase, or make a wall unit or a free-standing one out of wooden shelves bought at a lumberyard and fitted to your space. You're afraid you might have to move? Books are easy to pack and, although they are bulky, they are not expensive to mail because there is a book rate that is much cheaper than ordinary parcel post. They are easy to store, too. Books can be sold individually or in lots, they can be auctioned off, they can be traded, or they can be donated to your favorite college, university, library, or charity for a tax deduction. And in the meantime, you will have had the pleasure of their company.

THE DIFFERENCE BETWEEN COLLECTING AND ACCUMULATING

What makes the collector different from the accumulator? The accumulator buys or is given books and keeps them in a haphazard way, never really aware of what is there. The difference is really *awareness*. In a sense, this is the theme of this entire book: first, how to become aware of yourself in regard to what you are, and then how to collect books that will reflect your personality. Later on, as you discover more of yourself, your collection will grow in relation to this expanding awareness. In each of us, there is a treasure. Unfortunately, for most of us this treasure is buried, at least partially. An important aim of collecting is to uncover these gems within each of us; collecting can be one of the paths in this marvelous journey.

WHAT TO COLLECT

There are as many types of books to collect as there are collectors. The most important factor in choosing the type of book you wish to collect is your own interest at the time you begin. Most of you already have a favorite field, even if you aren't aware of it yet. Walk over to your bookshelves. The clue might be right there. Look at the books critically. Which books really turn you on? If a fire broke out, which ones would you save?

Pick the volumes up, look at each book, read the title page

and perhaps the pages the book falls open to. Ask yourself, "Does this book have a special meaning to me?"

A helpful guide is, did you buy the books or were they given to you? Those that you selected will usually have a more personal attraction.

Perhaps you'll notice a preponderance of one subject or type of book. Why were you attracted to these books? Most likely, they express a basic interest or motivation on your part. Many people collect the subjects of their fantasies, as can be seen by the popularity of "girlie" magazines and erotic art. I myself collect fantasy as expressed artistically in the works of the sixteenth-century Italian artists and the modern surrealists, dadaists, metaphysicians, and others.

I also collect printed ephemera—manifestos, invitations, postcards, tickets, and so forth—which are typographically beautiful as well as significant to twentieth-century art. I am attracted to ephemeral pieces because they were originally intended to be used for the moment and then thrown away—like human beings, who are ephemeral when measured against time. Preserving and displaying ephemeral things makes them *objets trouvés*, discovered objects put to a surprising use, and gives them a stature that was never intended. For me and for other ephemerists, this rescue operation may be a way of staving off our own mortality and trying to extend our presence in the world just a little bit longer.

Another approach to choosing a subject is to act on the feelings you have but have never dared to express or acknowledge; the type of misty area you talk about like this: "If I had the time, I would ————" (you fill it in); or, "If I had the money, I would ————" (fill this in, too); or, "I would like to surround myself with books that are ————." Could the missing words here be "beautiful, with lots of illustrations?" Could the blank be filled by a subject, say butterflies, or cars, or airplanes, or trains? It may be miniature books, or large books—called folios—that you can immerse yourself in, or books that help you in your work or hobby. Or ————; you fill it in.

COLLECTING AS SELF-DISCOVERY

What I am trying to do is to make you stop and think; or better still, feel. What was the long gone-by day, or event, or subject that took you away from reality and made you forget your surroundings, that took you instead to the enchanters' domain? This is the essence of personal collecting—not what is the current best seller or was made into the most popular movie, but what is the most pleasurable memory.

Let me give you an example. When I was in the sixth grade, I was given a textbook with illustrated endpapers. The endpapers fascinated me. The illustration, spreading from the inside front cover to the free endpaper next to it, showed a boy and girl surrounded by various means of transportation—buses, cars, trucks, ships of all types, blimps, planes, gliders, balloons, seaplanes. Under the picture was the caption "Progress through Transportation."

I never forgot the picture or its caption. Twenty years later when I was picnicking on Randall's Island, I suddenly found myself smack in the middle of that scene. Boats plied back and forth on the East River, trucks, cars, and buses passed by on the Triboro Bridge, a train moved parallel to them, and overhead flew aircraft landing and taking off from LaGuardia Airport. "That's it!" I screamed out loud to my kids. "That's the scene I've been waiting for, for over twenty years!" And I stood up and stared at it for what seemed like hours, while my thoughts slipped back to the sixth grade and the book that had captivated me then and still held sway over me years later.

This type of experience is what collecting should be, if possible. Without it, the magic is absent, and collecting can become less binding, so to speak. Listen to your feelings, memories, and intuitions; what comes out is what you should collect. If you already have a field or subject area, this approach may give you a new insight as to why you have chosen it.

If you can incorporate the magic and pleasure into your collection, you will have a happier time collecting, and your discoveries will be more personal and more pleasurable as a result.

In the eighteenth century, an English gentleman was known by his clothes and his library. If you met him on the street, his clothes told you that he was a gentleman. If you were invited to his home, the books lining his shelves added to your knowledge of his character. Today, this isn't true to the same extent. A person's library isn't always the key to his or her personality. Book clubs, best seller lists, and popular movies and magazines, rather than our own needs, desires, and fantasies, all too often influence our choices. We spend too much time looking for advice on how to collect and what to buy rather than looking inward, asking ourselves whether we need, want, or care about a book, title, or subject.

You must discover what relationship with the printed word or image adds both depth and a new dimension to yourself. View yourself as a house with many unfurnished rooms. If you furnish them yourself without the help of a decorator, then what you select will be both personal and satisfying, and the rooms will add to the character of the house. You will be the master. You will know when a particular room is furnished, and when to change the decor.

This approach may be a little scary for you to begin with, so I am going to outline some others that may be easier for starters. But promise me that, as soon as you can, you will think about what I have said and start to explore your own inner world as a subject for collecting.

COLLECTING BOOKS ABOUT YOUR PROFESSION

Most of us work for a living, and if we're fortunate, what we do interests us. You may already have a small library of books relating to your occupation. These books probably enhance your profession or explain, guide, or inform your practice. Whatever your profession, you can be sure that there are hundreds of books, periodicals, and catalogues that can help you in it. If your job really turns you on, you may also want to collect books on its history. Chances are there are many of them. A nice thing about collecting books about your profession is that their cost may be tax deductible, if they enhance your professional standing.

To find out the titles of books about your profession, consult a bibliography relating to your field. Or go to your nearest library, whether it is a public library, college or university library, or technical library, and ask the librarian to show you books pertaining to your field. For starters, look through the available material and see if there are particular areas within the field that hold more than routine interest for you. These areas can then become the ones you collect.

COLLECTING BOOKS ABOUT YOUR HOBBIES

Most of us like a change of pace after our work. Why not collect books about your hobbies? If you enjoy using your hands rather than your head, there are books relating to carpentry, auto repair, clocks, painting, sculpting, photography, astronomy, gardening, boating, travel, and so on. Sports are a very good field to look into, the general subject area as well as the individual sport—swimming, hiking, tennis, basketball, baseball, soccer, golf, running, flying, whatever. Don't confine yourself to how-to-do-it books about your sport or hobby. Look at the whole subject—the people who do it or did it, where it is done, its history, changes in it, technological inventions, and equipment and accessories. Each of these aspects, or a combination of two or more, can become a subject to collect. The possibilities are enormous. If you are starting, don't let yourself become overwhelmed by the profusion of titles. Concentrate on one subject, and little by little, as you feel more at ease with the field, enlarge on it.

COLLECTING BOOKS ABOUT YOUR HOMETOWN

Regionalism is another area for collecting. Americana—publications on and about America—is very popular now. But you can collect books on any community, town, city, county, state, or country—your own, or the place your parents of grandparents came from—or any region you are interested in. Your collection can be from almost any point of view: the way the region used to look—as in old maps and prints; its natural features—the apple orchards, vineyards, trees; its produce—crops or manufactured goods; its geographic location—if it's near the sea, shipping interests and boats, if on a river, the boats that plied the river, like the Mississippi steamboats, or flat barges; the city—its buildings, streets, views of the changes in urban planning, its restoration, its important monuments; the transportation changes—from carriages to trams to buses or subways, or the railroads that came there and perhaps no longer have any visible existence other than the stations; the fire department—its changes, personnel, equipment; the police; sanitation; tourist attractions—like Niagara Falls, or the Statue of Liberty, or even a district like Greenwich Village, where we are located.

Or try the human interest angle. The inhabitants of the area before Columbus ruined it. The famous people who lived there. Lincoln in Kentucky. The Mormons arriving in Utah. Explorers of the area—Hudson, De Soto, Lewis and Clark. The pioneers. The people who came to work here and returned home, and those who fled from oppression in the old country. The skills the immigrants brought—brewing to Milwaukee, sheepherding to Idaho, etc.

Or start a collection about deserted towns in the West, their history and days of glory and decay. Or Utopian settlements, like New Hope. Or cities with Greek and Roman names and their namesakes in the old world.

Or how about the arts, architecture, printing, and music in the area, and their development.

Or newspapers, periodicals, and books about the area, and their histories.

I could go on and on; but it's up to you to follow through on the suggestion that sparks your interest.

COLLECTING BOOKS ON AUTHORS, ARTISTS, OR OTHER PERSONALITIES

Many people are interested in collecting the works of a single author. Preferably the author has not only written books but has also been written about; in other words, there is a body of written information about the personality. So you can collect the author's own works in various editions and translations, anthologies where the author's works appear, and books and articles about the author. Many collectors like to collect first editions of the author's works— the first appearance of the book, in its most complete state, with the original dust wrapper. Many like to collect original material, such as the author's original manuscripts, letters by the author, postcards, signatures, and dedications the author made in books written by others, or the author's signature and inscriptions in his or her own works.

A related field is collecting books about artists—painters, sculptors, architects, dancers, musicians, composers, performers, film personalities, stage personalities, and, indeed, giants in every field. Collect their own books, books about them, catalogues of their exhibitions, or *oeuvre catalogues* which list all their works, movements that they initiated or were part of, and the places they worked in, lived in, and traveled to.

Experts in various fields are also collected. Critics who wrote about the artists and authors. Personalities who were part of an art movement. People who knew famous people. Biographers— Boswell on Johnson, Sabartes on Picasso, Jones on Freud. Americans love this type of book because most of us aren't quite sure that something's worthwhile until a so-called authority gives it his or her seal of approval. Why can't we read the author's work first, then see what other people have to say about it—and if their opinions don't agree with ours, so much the better.

COLLECTING ESCAPE LITERATURE

What do you read to get away from it all? Why not collect that type of book? What comes to mind first is the mystery or detective novel, or science fiction. Too many so-called highbrows look down on this type of reading and collecting. I do not. I think that any book that carries one off into the enchanters' domain is fulfilling one of the most important functions of reading. That is what makes a book so eternal and individual. My wife reads mysteries as if they were going out of style, and at the most unlikely times—when she is doing the dishes, taking a shower, putting on her make-up, or doing her laundering. The books she reads this way are paperbacks, of course, but they serve their purpose. I wouldn't recommend that you do the same with more expensive editions, but using your collection to provide relaxation or a temporary sanctuary from a harried and pressing world is certainly reason enough to collect this type of book, or, for that matter, to collect at all.

Each of us has a subject that can transport us from the ordinary to a private world of our own. For some it is the mystery or detective story; for others it may be adventure or seafaring novels, gothics or romances, supernatural tales, science fiction, or fantasy. Some people watch television to relax, but if you prefer reading, then old movies, situation comedies, sports events, news, and other television-type fare all can be found in book form; and, unlike television, books can be enjoyed when you want, where you want, and how you want. And no commercials—the breaks are yours.

Another escape area is nostalgia—a growing subject, and for good reason. We love to reminisce about the past—our own, our families', our friends'; the times grow better with age, like good wine. One can collect a whole era by selecting its printed matter, its personalities, events, highlights, music, art, fashion, and literature. When the selection has personal associations for you, the pleasure is more immediate.

To help you break into the field, use a guide. Literary guides are numerous. Many take the shape of anthologies: *Selections from the Best . . . , An Introduction to . . . , A Survey of the Most Important . . . , A Sampler of . . . , A Treasury of . . . , The History of . . . , The Complete Account of . . . .* You can fill in the subject or area, era or epoch, time or place. You needn't purchase these volumes. Borrow them from a friend, or the library, and look through them to see which of the samples appeal to you. And don't go about this research in a grim way; enjoy the trip, open up to it, let the parts talk to you, let them reach you so that you can respond in a relaxed, open, natural way. If you are uptight and worried about what you are doing, the results will be negative.

COLLECTING BOOKS ABOUT BOOKS

For the true booklover, perhaps no area is quite as satisfying as books about books. Included in this area are books on penmanship or calligraphy, the art of skillfully transcribing the sound or word on paper, so that the work looks as beautiful as it sounds; books on typography and book design; books on paper; books on printing techniques; books on the history of printing; books on writing and editing; and so on. Within each of these broad categories, there are smaller fields that may form the basis for a collection.

A book that may give you some ideas of what to collect in this area is *Printing and the Mind of Man*, a fine catalogue of an exhibition held in London in 1963, at the British Museum and Earls Court. The exhibition was a delight because it included the machines, tools, and equipment of printing as well as many important books. The catalogue is chockful of ideas for the present or future collector.

COLLECTING ILLUSTRATED BOOKS

Related to books about books are books and periodicals with illustrations or with original graphics. Sometimes the artists have collaborated on the book with the writer or publisher; in other cases, the illustrations were not originally planned for the text. Illustrated books and periodicals are usually grouped under the heading of "the art of the book."

The twentieth century has provided us with a new sensibility to the art of the book. From the late works of Cézanne on to op art, we have been growing accustomed to seeing space in painting from a two-dimensional view rather than the three-dimensional one developed in the Renaissance. The "view through the window" and into the universe or cosmos has been replaced with the two-dimensional wall or flat surface. The cubists imitated the lettering of mastheads or even incorporated pieces of newspapers into their paintings to give their works their flatness and aura of immediacy. Kurt Schwitters's *Merz* collages were named after the German newspaper *Commerz*, whose title he cut up to fit his design.

But nothing is more two-dimensional than a book page, with its flat surface decorated with print, text, and illustrations. Nothing is cleaner and more spacious than a well-designed layout—the *mis en page*, as the French call it. What a lovely collage! The design of books in this century has developed right along with twentieth-century art. The artists, photographers, sculptors, and typographers who have contributed to book design include almost all the giants of the twentieth century, from Appel to Zwart. And for me Matisse's masterpiece *Jazz* is the highest expression of modern book design.

The art of the book is a superb field of collecting. Here one experiences a wonderful unity of all the elements of the graphic arts—printing, fine paper, typography, layout, design, color, texture, and language. And keep in mind that illustration should not be dependent on the text but on the ability of the artist to enhance the text with a design that adds another dimension to the written word. The illustration combines with the text to give the work an added value, but if the text were absent the illustration would remain a work of art by itself.

COLLECTING BOOKS FOR THEIR APPEARANCE

All books look good, in my opinion, but some have features that appeal to a person's individual sense of beauty. For some collectors, this may be books with beautiful illustrations. For others, it may be books with beautiful bindings: a bookseller I know in Copenhagen collects books bound in red leather and shelves them together so that they create a large red square on his living room wall, which he finds very satisfying to look at. Other collectors look for books of a certain size, such as miniatures or, at the other extreme, elephant folios.

Many collectors, including me, who have other subject areas, nevertheless often buy books because they look or feel "right." The volume has "weight," not in the pound sense, but in the sense that when you hold it and look through it you feel it to be very attractive. I have bought many books like this, just because I like the feel of them. The parts—the cover, the text, the printing, the illustrations—all unite to form a very sympathetic whole. The subject area may not be just right, but the feeling is.

This is all very personal. It depends on what gives you pleasure, what makes you smile, what satisfies you. And that is for me a most worthwhile subject to collect.

COLLECTING FOR INVESTMENT

As I said in Chapter 1, the inflationary spiral means that the price of most books increases with time. So the books and periodicals you buy now are almost certain to increase in value, whatever they are. The books you thought were cheap, the books you paid fair market for, and the books you paid too much for will all look like bargains five or ten years from now.

But remember, one rule of thumb is the more you spend on a given item, the more it will appreciate. Try to buy the best examples offered in your field, the most beautifully printed, with the best texts and in the best possible condition. Concentrate on books that are out of print; you have to wait longer for an in-print book to appreciate in value.

Specific types of books and periodicals that have shown the most growth in recent years are photography; modern illustrated books (twentieth and late nineteenth century); books with color plates (seventeenth through nineteenth centuries); first editions, American and English; Americana; and twentieth-century art and literary movements—for example, futurism, surrealism, dadaism, art deco, constructivism, and suprematicism. What books will show most growth in the future? That depends on future fads and fashions.

Another good area for investment is based on the nature of inflation itself. When money shrinks, durable goods increase in worth. So more and more people are investing in "hard money" items like real estate, homes, furniture, paintings, jewelry, gold, precious metals, oriental rugs, sculpture, prints, and books. These investors want to improve their knowledge, their expertise, and the provenance of their acquisitions or collections. What better way than in buying books on these subjects? Books will enhance the value of the other collection as well as the collector's knowledge of the field. So books on collectibles are another area for collecting, and good out-of-print, scarce, or rare books in the fields of your collecting will provide a double pleasure.

Another rule of collecting for investment is to buy books on a particular subject or area of interest, because the total collection will then become worth more than the sum of its parts; that is, the value of the collection will grow at a faster pace than each individual title or volume. As in a mutual fund, you won't have to worry about the individual item's track record. Some books will go up faster than others, but the unity of the collection will enhance the total.

That the collection takes on a life of its own can be seen a little clearer, perhaps, in a university library. Some twenty-five years ago, Jens Nyholm at Northwestern University began collecting books and periodicals on twentieth-century radical art and literature—futurism, expressionism, dada, surrealism, constructivism, and so on. Mr. Nyholm established an excellent relationship with the book trade. He visited the dealers, told them what he was interested in, and asked them to offer material to him in these areas and send him advance copies of their catalogues. Within a few years, offers, catalogues, and letters were pouring into the library, and the collection really took off. The momentum continued under Mr. Nyholm's successors, Dr. Richard Press and now R. Russell Maylone. At present the collection is one of the best and most prominent in the world.

What are the dynamics involved? When you start shaping a collection, you are buying the works that are important—the key works of an author, movement, or area. You get to know the supporting literature, the reference works, the published bibliographies, and so on, and little by little you become a *maven*, or, as *The New York Times* says in its obituaries, "an authority on the subject." Slowly but surely you begin noticing footnotes and references cited, then bibliographies. You notice the names and places mentioned in the index and the sources, and you follow these up. You note what you already have and what you would like to have. The pieces of the puzzle begin to fit. They fall into shape, and what was only a small group of books begins to form the nucleus of a collection.

The center that holds it all together, the glue, so to speak— is you. You are the mason who searches for and eventually finds the missing pieces. You have become the conscious collector; you have grown from the passive or perhaps unconscious picker to the avid consumer, held in check only by your monetary and time limitations. You are now a builder. You feel the full pleasures of the motivated, dedicated, and inspired collector. This building, this pursuit, this dedicated search is what makes for great collections. That is why the collection is worth more than the sum of its parts; you have endowed it with your personality, your vision, and your taste. It is indeed your collection.

If you eventually dispose of it, you will find that the effort, knowledge, and awareness you have brought to the collection have added to its value.

CHAPTER 3

Starting Out

Once you have chosen a subject or area that you think might be fun, then the real excitement of collecting begins. Now you can get ready to buy. But first there are some important matters to clear up. The first step is to put the books you already have in order, so that you can see what's there and what isn't, and so that you'll have a system set up for storing and finding the books you buy in the future.

HOW TO CATALOGUE YOUR BOOKS

Go through your books and periodicals and decide which are important to you. Don't worry about it, just relax and take your time with each volume. The decision isn't necessarily final. What you are doing is separating those books that have a certain mystique from those that do not. This doesn't imply that what remains is of no worth, or that you have to discard it; it only means that for now the books without that special pizazz aren't as important to you as the others. In the future, they may change their status as your tastes change or grow.

Put the books that are important to you in one pile, shelf, or carton, and those that are not in another. Arrange each pile alphabetically by authors, artists (in the case of illustrated books),

27

or subjects; I prefer to do it by authors. Now you are going to
start to catalogue your books.

Cataloguing has been called the intellectual side of the book
business and the library profession. Many people make a career
of it. Some people love the methodology itself. Others appreciate
this opportunity to hold, examine, and browse through the book.
For others, cataloguing is simply a pain in the neck; but it must
be done because it provides an exact record of all the books and
periodicals in your possession. It's a form of inventory control,
important for future buying and selling and for tax records. For
library patrons it is an essential way of locating information; for
booksellers it is a step in the preparation of catalogues, which
are offerings from their stock.

There are various methods of cataloguing. If you are a stickler
for methodology, you might want to buy *Anglo-American Cataloguing Rules*, a book prepared by the American Library Association
(ALA), the Library of Congress, the Library Association, and the
Canadian Library Association, and published by the ALA in 1967.
But I don't think that it is really that important for you. What
is important is to devise a consistent system of cataloguing that
will grow and be helpful to you in keeping track of your collection.

It's best to do your cataloguing on index cards, one card for
each item in your collection, so that you can add new acquisitions
in alphabetical order. Use blank index cards if you are going to
type the information, and either blank or ruled cards if you are
going to handwrite the information. My inventory is listed on
3 × 5 inch index cards. Whether I buy a single volume or a
large collection, I catalogue each book on a separate 3 × 5 inch
index card. Each card contains the following information:

Author. Last name first, then first name, middle name or initial.
Title of the book. Full title as it appears on the title page, not on the
dust wrapper or half-title page. Then subtitle, if any.
Place of publication. City, if given, and country. If no information
is given, then mark "n.p." for "no place"; or if no place of publication

is mentioned but you know the place from other sources, write the place in parentheses—for example, "(New York)."

Publisher. (If privately printed, then the person or association the book was published for.)

Date. The date is usually on the bottom of the title page, or on the verso of the title page; or, if the volume is a limited edition, the date may appear in the colophon (inscription or emblem at the end of the book). If no date is given, then mark "n.d." for "no date"; or, if you know the date from other sources, write it in parentheses.

Edition. If stated, write it after the date: "1st ed.," "2nd ed.," or whatever. If it is a limited edition, mention the number of the copy (often written in ink in limited edition books) and the kind of paper or other features that distinguish it from the regular edition.

Number of pages. Include blank leaves, advertising matter, etc.

Number of plates, if illustrated. Here we make a distinction between the illustrations in the text, which we list as text illustrations ("text ills.") and plates outside of the main body of the text, usually printed on coated paper or a different stock from the text, which are called *hors texte* ("h.t."). If the plates are colored, we mention the fact.

Size. For the beginner, only four sizes are important. Later on you can get more precise if you wish, and measure the volume with a ruler in inches or centimeters. The four important sizes are folio, quarto, octavo, and duodecimo, which are written in dealers' catalogues as F (for folio), 4to (for quarto), 8vo (for octavo), and 12mo (for duodecimo). A folio is roughly 13 inches long; quarto, 10 to 13 inches; octavo, 7 to 9 inches—most books nowadays, except art books, are octavo; duodecimo, 6 to 7 inches. These sizes are approximate. If you do measure your books in centimeters or inches, list the height first, then the width (for example, 11 × 8 1/2 in.).

Binding. The material the book is bound in: cloth ("cl."), boards ("bds."), stiff cardboard, wrappers ("wr."), stiff paper, or paper as in paperbacks.

Condition. The state of wear of your book, described in terms such as fine, mint, very good, good, fair, and poor (a reading or working copy). It may take a little time for you to work out what condition your book is in.

Shelf number. This number belongs on the bottom of the card, in the lower left corner. It refers to where you keep the book. If you have a bookcase, you should mark each shelf with a little sticker that can easily be removed if necessary. On each sticker, write either a number or a letter of the alphabet. Numbers are better if you have or are planning to have a large collection, because in a short time you might need more than twenty-six shelves. If you decide to use the alphabet, then try to shelve the authors alphabetically in the shelf bearing their letter. Within each shelf, arrange the books alphabetically by author as well, from left to right. If you have two or more books by the same author, arrange them alphabetically by title.

Buying data. On the lower right-hand side, note the dealer, person, or library you bought the book from; the date you bought it; and the price, preferably in code. (See Chapter 6 on how to compose a code.)

Periodicals (magazines or journals) should be catalogued according to the *Union List of Serials*, available at the library.

Here is a sample of a book catalogue card:

LUCAS, E. Louise. *Art Books: A Basic Bibliography on the Fine Arts.* Greenwich, Connecticut. N.Y. Graphic Society, 1968 (2nd ed.). 245 p., 8vo, cl., good.

L   Minters 5/78 $X

On the top of the card, indicate in pencil the degree of interest that the title holds for you. A simple way to do this is by numbering the cards from 1 through 4. No. 1 is the most interesting, no. 2 is less so, no. 3 is still less, and no. 4 is undecided. If your priorities change, you can always erase the number.

On the back (verso) of the card, in pencil, you can keep track of the prices the book reaches at auctions and the prices it's listed for in booksellers' catalogues; and when you note these prices, always note the date and place so that you have a record of the way the prices change.

Now you can alphabetize all your cards, and place your books on the proper shelves (without regard to whether they're from the "interesting" or "uninteresting" pile, since this information is now on the cards). I keep my cards in file cabinets, but until your collection becomes really large, you don't need to go to this expense. When you buy the index cards, buy a box of ten packages; then you can use the box to store the completed cards in. Also, be sure to buy an alphabetical index, so that you can keep your cards in alphabetical order.

Cataloguing may seem like a lot of work in the beginning, but you'll thank me in the long run, because if you wish to sell or trade the item in the future, the card will contain all the information you need to charge a fair price. (If you do sell an item, be sure to keep the card, as I do, and enter the date of the sale, the person or library who bought the item, the price you sold it for, and your original cost. This will be your record for the Internal Revenue, since the sale should be reported if you made a profit—the difference between what you paid for the book and your expenses, such as postage, insurance, billing, etc.—minus what you sold it for.)

If you have a lot of books to catalogue, don't feel discouraged or overwhelmed. Just start, and in time you will have catalogued your whole collection. Remember, most libraries and booksellers, including me, are from six months to a year behind in cataloguing the books they have purchased. I have a hundred shelves filled with uncatalogued items, and I'm working on them all the time. I must confess, though, that although I haven't yet catalogued these books on 3 × 5 cards, I have a slip in each volume with the name of the person or dealer or library that I bought the book from and the date and price, so that I won't forget; when I get to the item, all the information is there, ready to be transferred to the index card. Once you get started, this procedure will become habit forming, and as you purchase new books, you will catalogue them before you shelve them. And as your collection grows, you will replace the cardboard index box with a metal one, and then a pair, and so on.

If you're just beginning to collect, I envy you. Sometimes I have the fantasy of selling all my stock, catalogued and uncatalogued, and starting afresh with just one book, and slowly and methodically building the collection until there are enough books to be listed in a catalogue, and then selling the collection en bloc to a rich collector; and then starting all over again. This fantasy grabs me whenever I buy a large collection and have to start cataloguing it while hundreds of my previous uncatalogued items sit there staring at me, resentful that their turn has been delayed again. But listen, we are all human, and the gems in any collection are always first to be catalogued or sold.

Anyway, starting fresh or not, the next step in collecting is discovering what is available and where to get it.

THE BOOK WORLD'S PERIODICALS

Reading the various periodicals put out by and for the book trade is a painless way of finding out what's going on in your specialty and at the same time becoming immediately involved with the events and personalities of the book world.

First of all, I recommend a subscription to the *AB Bookman's Weekly*—the *AB*, for short—a weekly periodical that lists books wanted and books for sale and includes articles on the book trade, book reviews, business notes, obituaries, publishers' advertisements, catalogue offers, auction house announcements, and advertisements of suppliers to the trade—binders, printers, restorers, appraisers, and manufacturers of goods needed for the preservation and upkeep of books. Jacob Chernofsky, publisher of the *AB*, like his predecessor, Sol Malkin, is always in evidence at book fairs and other important happenings, taking notes, snapping pictures, and interviewing people; so the *AB*'s coverage of the book world is up to date and extensive.

Only bookdealers can advertise in the "Books Wanted" sections of the *AB*; check these columns to see if any of them want the books you wish to dispose of (for information on how to answer these ads, see Chapter 10). You can also sell your books through the "Books for Sale" sections—anyone can advertise in those; and also check "Books for Sale" to locate books you want to buy.

To subscribe to the *AB*, write to: The Publisher, *AB Bookman's Weekly*, P.O. Box AB, Clifton, NJ 07015. The cost is $30 a year. Single issues are $2 each, or $3 for special issues, if you want to see for yourself before committing yourself to a subscription. If the price is too high for you at this time, then maybe you can arrange to share the cost with another collector; or, if you know a bookseller who subscribes, perhaps he or she will keep the old copies and pass them on to you, although they may be too marked up or you may get them too late to do you much good.

With a subscription to the *AB*, you also get a free copy of the *AB Bookman's Yearbook*; without the subscription, it is available from the same publisher for $7.50, or $5 for each of its two parts. The *Yearbook* is also available at libraries, where it is kept in the reference section. It is an important reference book for you because, in Part II, it contains a section called "The O.P. Market," which lists out-of-print bookdealers according to their specialties. If I get requests for titles not in my subject area, I look up the specialists in that area and send them a want list, which is a listing of the books I need. You can do the same. You can also write to the dealers in your subject area and ask to be put on their mailing lists. The *Yearbook* also contains advertisements, and some dealers may offer catalogues that you'd be interested in sending away for.

There are a couple of other American publications which you should also look into. *Book Collector's Market* (*BCM*) is a bi-monthly magazine edited by Denis Carbonneau and published by The Moretus Press, Inc. *BCM* covers auctions, book fairs, new dealers and their specialties, and personalities in the book trade. It also features columns on first editions, auctions, fine printing and small presses, prints and illustrated books, book collecting trends, and graphics conservation. The address for subscriptions is P.O. Box 3128,

Shiremanstown, PA 17011. A year's subscription is $16.50 for
individuals; single copies are $3.50 each.

The *Book-Mart*, edited by David G. Maclean and published
by Americana Books, is a monthly journal dealing mostly with
Americana and American authors. It contains checklists of works
with suggested values, book reports, bookdealers' and collectors'
wants, bookdealers' advertisements, books for sale, and calendars
of events of interest to bookpeople (fairs, auctions, etc.). The
mailing address is P.O. Box 243, Decatur, IN 46733. One year's
subscription is $8.50 via first-class mail, or $4 via third-class
mail; single copies are 40¢ each.

Other important journals are published in Great Britain,
France, Italy, and Germany. If you are collecting books that were
published in those countries, or subject areas relating to them—
authors, artists, printing, views, travels, for example—you should
familiarize yourself with these journals.

In Great Britain there are a few journals that might be of
interest to you. As with the American ones, you may write for
individual copies for examination before subscribing if you can't
find a copy in a library near your home.

The British journal most similar to the *AB* is a weekly published
by Fudge & Co., Ltd., called the *Bookdealer*. It contains an "Author
Interest Index," which is a list of authors whose works people
(mainly dealers) are interested in purchasing; a books for sale
section; announcements of local book fairs; announcements of
books relating to the book trade and reference works; dealers' ads;
and suppliers' ads. The address is Sardinia House, Sardinia Street,
London, WC2A 3NW, and the price of a yearly subscription is
£7.50.

The Clique is the oldest journal of the antiquarian book trade,
having started in 1890. This weekly contains sections on books
wanted and books for sale, but subscriptions are available only
to the trade. However, you might look for a copy when you are
in England, or you might ask a British dealer to pass on a copy

that he or she no longer needs with the next order he or she sends you.

There are two British journals especially for the collector. The *Book Collector*, an illustrated quarterly, is available for $24 a year from 3 Bloomsbury Place, London WC1A 2QA. Each issue contains "Bibliographical Notes and Queries"; "Uncollected Authors"; "Contemporary Collectors"; "Portrait of a Bibliophile": a discussion of a single important book; book reviews; reports on sales, catalogues, exhibitions, and other topical matters: and advertisements from antiquarian booksellers and auction houses throughout the world. The *Antiquarian Book Monthly Review*, 30 Cornmarket Street, Oxford OX1 3EY, includes "American Viewpoint," "Book Chats," trade notes, auction announcements, catalogue announcements, and advertisements from booksellers, publishers, and auction houses. The subscription price is $18 a year.

A new British publication, the *Bookdealers' and Collectors' Yearbook and Diary*, will be published every December by the Sheppard Press, P.O. Box 42, Russell Chambers, Covent Garden, London WC2E. The price is $6 a year, and the contents include articles, reviews, and a diary of events for the forthcoming year.

If you are collecting French books, printed matter, or ephemera, you should get a copy of *Bulletin du Bibliophile*, 18 Rue Dauphine, 75006 Paris. Four numbers are published annually at NF 130 for foreigners (about $31). In a typical number, the editorials and articles on rare books are of general interest to the serious collector. Two important regular features are a chronicle of events in the book world and a list of catalogues published by booksellers affiliated with the International League of Antiquarian Booksellers (ILAB), with a listing of the subjects covered in each catalogue. If a particular subject is of interest to you, you can obtain the catalogue by writing to the dealer.

You never know what will result from an ad in a journal like this. In 1963, I advertised in *SLAM*, the French journal published by the Syndicat National de la Librarie Ancienne et Moderne, which is now combined with the *Bulletin du Bibliophile*. I was looking for single numbers and runs of French little magazines such as *Action, Commerce,* and *Plans*. I received an answer not from Paris but from Kentucky. Professor Walter Langlois, then teaching in the Department of French at the University of Kentucky was also looking for certain numbers of these journals. Seeing my ad, he had reasoned that if I was looking for some numbers, I must already have others in stock, which he could use to fill in the gaps in his holdings. I did. That started two beautiful relationships—with him and with the library; both still continue, although Professor Langlois is now at the University of Wyoming. I hope you establish similar relationships with other collectors and with booksellers and libraries.

In Italy, the *Gazzettino Librario* is the publication of the Italian antiquarian book trade. The address is Via J. Nardi, 6. 50132 Florence, Italy, and the price is L. 8.500 (about $11) a year. The journal is published monthly and contains a listing of catalogues and publications received from American, British, Italian, and other European antiquarian booksellers, a books wanted section, a books for sale section, advertisements of Italian antiquarian booksellers with their specialties, and announcements by publishers of forthcoming books. Most important, on the inside covers there is a geographical listing of booksellers who are members of the Italian antiquarian association (Associazione Librari Antiquari d'Italia), which is very helpful if you are traveling through the country and wish to stop off and visit some dealers.

Germany has a publication, *Börsenblatt für den Deutschen Buchhandel*, which is similar to *Publishers Weekly* because it is really for the new-book trade; but it has a supplement, "Angebotene unde Gesuchte Bücher," that can be purchased separately and is for antiquarians. The supplement lists wanted/offered books and includes dealers' advertisements. The address is Buchhandler-Vereinigung GmbH, 6 Frankfurt am Main 1, Grosser Hirschgraben 17/21, Germany.

BOOK WORLD DIRECTORIES

It's important for you to know who the out-of-print booksellers are. A list of booksellers who are members of the Antiquarian Booksellers' Association of America, Inc. (ABAA) can be obtained free from the Association at 50 Rockefeller Plaza, New York, NY 10020, telephone 212–757–9395; enclose a self-addressed stamped envelope.

If you are going to collect in a serious way—and frankly I don't see how your collection can develop otherwise—then you will need the *International Directory of Antiquarian Booksellers*. The sixth edition was published in 1977. It can be purchased from the ABAA for $10. The directory provides a worldwide guide to antiquarian booksellers, who are listed geographically, by specialty, and alphabetically. The dealers listed are members of their national antiquarian associations. For each country, the business hours and legal holidays are listed, which, believe me, is a real help if you are planning a trip to that country and want to make sure that you will find the firm open on arrival. The directory also lists the firms' telephone numbers, their cable addresses, their owners or managers, and even their banks. Tucked into a pocket on the inside back cover are maps showing where the antiquarian booksellers in Amsterdam and Copenhagen are located. Usually other cities have similar maps that you can get when you are there—Paris has a splendid one, and in New York, ABAA's Middle Atlantic Chapter (MAC) has published a map that has Manhattan dealers on one side, and dealers in the other boroughs and the neighboring areas of Long Island, New York State, Connecticut, New Jersey, Eastern Pennsylvania, and Western Massachusetts on the verso. If you are planning a trip abroad, write to the country's national association and ask for the map of the city or cities you plan to visit. Take the *International Directory* with you—it is small and lightweight—and keep all the maps tucked into the back pocket.

The Clique—the British Journal available only to the trade—

publishes an *Annual Directory of Booksellers in the British Isles Specialising in Antiquarian and Out-of-Print Books*, which is available to everyone. Write to 75 World's End Road, Handsworth Wood, Birmingham B20 2NS, England; the price is $5. The directory will be helpful if you visit Great Britain—a great place to visit and buy books. It's fun to visit the dealers there and get to know them personally. Try rural England; it's well served by British Rail as well as modern roads and offers the collector an opportunity to visit the country, see the sights, visit local dealers, stay in small inns, and eat and drink in the local pubs. For leisurely browsing, try to arrange your trip for the spring or fall, not in the height of the summer tourist season. This rule holds true for the Continent as well, where most shops and firms are closed in August and even part of July.

For German-language booksellers, see the *Adressbuch für den deutschsprachigen Buchhandel* (the *Directory of the German-language Book Trade*), available from Buchhändler-Vereinigung GmbH, Adressbuch, Redaktion, Postfach 2404, D-6000 Frankfurt 1, Germany. Ask for Volume 2, "Booksellers"; it lists the booksellers in Germany, Austria, and Switzerland, as well as those in other countries who sell German books. Volume 2 costs DM 46 (about $24).

There is also an *International Directory of Book Collectors*, published by the Trigon Press, 117 Kent House Road, Beckenham, Kent BR 31JJ, England, at $30. It includes a free entry form; if you are a bona fide collector, your name can be included in the next edition, and you will probably be contacted by other collectors in your area of collecting and put on the mailing lists of booksellers, publishers, remainder houses, and suppliers to the trade. The directory also lists bookpeople's societies that you may wish to join. Part of the fun of collecting is sharing your interests with others—writing and talking to other collectors and to booksellers and librarians, attending auctions, visiting shops, going to book fairs, and joining societies and clubs.

USING THE LIBRARY

The library is a wonderful place to go for the information you need in starting out and to continue to use as you become more and more informed and involved with your collection. The reference section and the reference librarian are most important for your investigations.

For general reference, most libraries have such important reference tools as the *Art Index*, the *Union List of Serials*, *Books in Print*, *The New York Times Book Review*, the *New York Review of Books*, auction records, encyclopedias, bibliographies, and biographies. Libraries also subscribe to specialized journals such as the *Library Journal* and *Publishers Weekly*, which contain information on new books, reference works, and book reviews.

For reference sources directly relating to your field, tell the librarian what you are collecting. A professional reference librarian will know what books and periodicals are available in your field and will put you in contact with them. Also look up materials about authors, artists, or subjects in the library's catalogue, which is often in card form. Check the *Reader's Guide to Periodical Literature* for articles about your subject. Always take a pen and a pad, or preferably a package of index cards, to note the sources of your information. Note the information in the same way that you catalogue your books. After you locate the books or periodicals you want, borrow them; or read them in the library, if they don't circulate. If you want to examine a book that is not in the library's collection, you can request that it be borrowed from another branch. After you see the books, you can decide which ones you want to buy for yourself. Within a short time you will feel comfortable in the library, know the staff, and look forward to spending the time finding out about your subject.

If you live near a college or university library, you are lucky. Most college and university libraries have special collections and excellent reference sections, so there is even more material available to you. Now, with security tight, it may be more difficult, but most colleges and universities will let you use their libraries if you talk to the librarian and tell him or her that you are a collector.

Join the library if it is a public one, or become a "friend" of the college or university library in your vicinity. It is well worth the expense, and without a doubt the library needs your support. As a friend or donor, you may receive bulletins and announcements and sometimes attend meetings and dinners. In the long run you will feel that you are a part of the library and will be treated as indeed a friend. The staff will extend themselves in a way that will surprise you. Nothing makes one feel as good as being relied upon and appreciated, especially in the profession one is trained in. If you recognize a person's expertise, he or she will usually go out of his or her way to help you find the material you are looking for.

The psychology of asking is a simple one. Be polite and patient. Come on in a human way, admitting what you do not know, and allowing the person who knows to tell you. Remember, collecting is like a chain. Each link you make is important, and the link with the librarian and the library is one of the most important of all.

USING THE BOOKSTORE

What I have said about the library and the librarian is also true for your neighborhood booksellers, whether they deal in antiquarian or new books or both; new books can be important reference tools for you. Introduce yourself to the proprietor, manager, and clerks. Give them your card—if you don't have any have some printed up—and tell them of your interests. Ask them if they have anything in stock for you; if your interests are still vague, perhaps they can suggest an area, subject, or author. Inspect the books they show you and decide whether you want to buy them for your collection or for reference. I spend several hundred dollars each year on my reference library, because I find it essential to keep up with the latest works in my specialty areas.

If you are far from a library, or if your library doesn't have *Books in Print*, whose value for you as a reference tool I'll talk about in Chapter 6, then you can look at it at the bookstore. You can find out if the work you are interested in is in print; if it is, the bookstore will order it for you if you wish.

Many bookstores, even those that deal exclusively in new books, will search for an out-of-print item if you ask them to. Some charge a nominal fee for this service, say $1 per title, but many don't. Most bookstores have a section with reduced prices on books that have been remaindered (see Chapter 7) or that aren't moving fast; always go through this section, because you can find some good buys in it.

PLANNING YOUR BOOK BUDGET

An important part of starting to collect is deciding how much money you are going to spend on your collection. There are expensive books and less expensive books. You can buy a lot or a little. What you spend for collecting should be surplus money— money that you can spend without having to sacrifice or cut into your living budget. Money to burn. Budget yourself so that you have taken care of all the essentials before you decide to put money into the collection. You will feel better about it, and the relationship you have with your suppliers and associates will be a happier one in the long run.

Set aside a certain amount per week or month for collecting. The amount needn't be large. I started my collection when I was in public school and got an allowance of 25¢ a week. I was in the fifth grade and was given the task of designing a mural on Latin America. I had seen some Diego Rivera reproductions at my Aunt Sarah's house, and I really loved them. I asked my father, who was an outdoor decorator with a studio in Greenwich Village, to help me find books on Rivera and other Mexican artists. We went to Fourth Avenue, which in the 1940s was a marvelous source of good out-of-print and second-hand books. I found a couple of books with colored plates that were just what I had in mind. I had trouble understanding some of the words, but the illustrations were marvelous, and I used them as an inspiration for the mural.

My collection continued to grow through high school and college. In fact, when I decided to become a bookseller, my first catalogue consisted of my own library; it was a painful experience to sell it, but a necessary one, considering that I started in business with just $200, borrowed from my father and a friend. It's harder to start out today with that small a sum, but it can be done if you are patient, have more time than money, and enjoy spending the time searching for books. Don't get discouraged. Concentrate on the present, stay within your budget, and the quest will be infinitely pleasurable and rewarding.

CHAPTER 4

Buying from Shops

Now we get to what I consider the most exciting part of collecting—buying the books. There are various sources for buying books: you can buy by mail, buy at auction, and so forth; and I'll discuss all of them, since you probably won't want to confine yourself to a single source. But let's start with buying from the antiquarian bookshop.

GETTING TO KNOW THE PROS

In a very short time you will, through personal discovery or through recommendations, references, advertisements, the directories I told you about in Chapter 3, or other sources, get to know the pros. These are the antiquarian bookdealers in your area or specialty, and they are extremely important for your collecting. They are the specialists who stock the books, periodicals, and other items in your field and who will most likely have or can get for you the titles you are interested in.

The first step in dealing with a specialist is to get to know him or her in person. If the firm isn't an open shop, call up and make an appointment. Ask if the owner or manager or specialist in your area will be in, and also if they have in stock at the present time items or collections that might be of interest to you.

Even if the shop is open to the public, it's a good idea to phone in advance and ask what would be the best time to view the books. Arrive on time, introduce yourself, and tell the person what you are collecting and the titles and/or subjects you are interested in. If the bookseller hasn't the time to help you, then don't insist on it unless you are visiting an out-of-town dealer or a dealer in a foreign country and your stay is limited to that particular day. In that case, tell the dealer that fact, and he or she might be more helpful.

Antiquarian bookdealers are by and large an individualistic lot. They are anarchists as much as capitalists, and almost the last of those small-business owners who can arrange their businesses to suit their personalities and conduct them according to their own whims. Sometimes their whim may be to behave as though they don't really need you or your business, but don't let this faze you. Remember, here is a person with years of experience, and knowledge and material that can be of tremendous help to you and your collection. Take advantage of it.

Do what dealers do when they go on a buying trip. When dealers visit a shop, they have more than one reason to be there. True, they want to buy good books at a good price, but they also want to see their colleagues, talk with them, and find out what is new in stock and what they might need in the future. They note the stock and the prices and find out what's coming up— a collection, a new catalogue, a new business venture, a move, a trip, whatever. They leave a list of titles or subject areas they are interested in. In short, they are keeping in touch.

On the whole, we dealers are a compatible group who buy and sell among ourselves and for the most part stay on good terms with one another. If we are helpful to our competitors, we certainly can and should be more so to our customers. Our colleagues, however, are experienced bookdealers and know the etiquette of buying and selling. You should, too, so that you can handle yourself like a pro as soon as possible.

SHOPPING ETIQUETTE

Your frame of mind and attitude toward the experience are of utmost importance when you visit antiquarian bookshops. Enter the shop with a positive, easy manner and a sense of humor. Remember always that you are there to look at and buy books, not to become involved with the dealer's personality or business practices. Be polite and easygoing, and keep your wits about you. Learn to say things in a positive way. For example, if you find that the prices are higher than you think they should be, note them without comment if they are important for you. If you find something that you really want and it is more than you wish to spend, ask if there is any chance of a small adjustment.

If the dealer refuses, then don't become negative in your attitude. If you haven't noticed it before, dealers are all a little *michuga*; otherwise they would not be in this profession. Many of them remind me of prima donnas, and I have learned over the years to approach them in a positive, casual, and humorous way, trying to understand their gigs.

The rewards are more than worth the effort. The majority will work with you, offer you items of interest when they get them, search for specific titles you want if they have a search service (and you should inquire about this), recommend items of interest for your collection whether they be reference works or collectibles, and in general guide you in your development as a collector. Don't shut off the pleasures and enjoyment of browsing and building your collection and knowledge. If a dealer is really obnoxious, the best thing to do is leave the shop. Do your business with that shop by mail or telephone in the future.

BROWSING WITH A PURPOSE

The art of browsing is an individual one. By that I mean it should conform to your style, method, manner, and personality. Browsing can add to your knowledge, lead to exciting discoveries of sleepers or really good items, allow you to compare prices, and help you in establishing a good relationship with bookdealers.

When you go browsing, it is good practice to carry a small notebook and pen or pencil for noting pertinent information for future reference—titles, prices, condition, and other facts relating to the books that you see. When you get home, copy the information onto a 3 × 5 index card so that it will be readily available for future reference; do this as soon as possible, while the notes are fresh in your mind and you can put them into the proper categories—author; title; subject; etc. Always date each entry so that you can later compare changes in price, interest, and relevance to your collection. There is nothing that will help your collection more than seeing and judging the books for yourself.

The first time you enter a shop that is devoted exclusively to out-of-print, scarce, and second-hand books, introduce yourself and ask if you may browse. Let the personnel know what areas, subjects, or authors you are interested in. They will direct you to the right shelves. Check the books there carefully, noting the prices and inspecting the items that look interesting. If you come across a book that is unknown to you, take the time to examine it thoroughly. Check the blurb and read the table of contents, the index, the references cited, and the bibliography. If there is something there that adds to your information, or if you feel that the book will be a plus to your collection, skim a few pages of the chapters that are of most interest to you or your collection. If you aren't sure that you want to buy the book, note the title in your pad for later consideration.

After you have covered the obvious sections of the shop, stop and think about what other areas or subjects may be related to your areas. For example, a specialty of mine is architecture, and Le Corbusier. I am always looking for good books on and by him. The logical places to look would be in the architecture or art sections, or under "Le Corbusier." But in the 1930s, the Studio of London published a book by Le Corbusier called *Aircraft*. So, with this in mind, I also ask dealers about aviation, or I look through the aviation section with the hope of finding the title there. It is such knowledge of interrelationships that you should develop, because it will help you broaden your collection.

Another area to look at is the miscellaneous or general section; it may prove to be a treasure. Most booksellers don't bother to sort those books that are out of their specialty into fine subdivisions; they simply haven't the time, or maybe the knowledge. So a good number of titles fall into the general area, and these usually are more reasonably priced than those that are placed within a subject category. The miscellaneous or general sections may be called by those names, or they may be labeled "non-fiction" or grouped alphabetically by author, artist, or subject.

After you have worked your way through all the above sections, if you haven't found anything that interests you go back to the owner, manager, or clerk and ask if there is a section on rare or more expensive books. If there is, ask to be shown that, too. Some dealers keep all expensive books (and what they consider expensive is relative to the general quality of the stock) in a separate area under lock and key. Check this section out. It may contain the more important titles for you.

Before you leave the shop, give the dealer your card and ask if he or she will notify you should items of interest to your collection come his or her way. Some dealers will; others don't want to, or don't work that way. If the dealer will, leave a list of the books you want. Ask if the shop issues catalogues; if it does, get on the mailing list. If it is a shop that specializes in your areas, then pay to receive the catalogues by first-class mail, since many important items will be sold long before you receive your catalogue by third-class mail or book rate. Many dealers will deduct the cost of the first-class postage from any item purchased from the catalogue.

Don't overlook bookshops that look formidable or that you think might be too expensive for you. I have always found reasonably priced books even in the most expensive-looking shops. It is good experience for you to browse (if permitted) in shops specializing in more expensive items, because you may not have the opportunity to see books of this type in lower-priced second-hand bookshops. Expensive shops usually will be more cautious in their initial dealings with you, so it is particularly important to phone beforehand and make an appointment to see the person there who specializes in your area. Ask to see specific titles or subjects, and be very careful in the way you handle the books. If you are overwhelmed with either their beauty or their prices, try not to show it. If the books are out of your price range, then simply pass them up.

Another important thing to keep in mind is to visit all bookshops regardless of their specialty, because bookdealers often buy collections en bloc, and some collections may contain items of interest for you that normally wouldn't be in that shop. You can stumble on good buys quite by chance, and just by being there at the right time you may even be able to purchase a small group of books in your area en bloc.

This happened to me in 1965. I was in Europe, ending my trip in London to coincide with the British antiquarian book fair, which at that time was held at the National Book League House. My Danish friend Ole Dam was in London, too, and we met at the fair on opening night. He suggested that we meet the next morning at the bookshop called Edwards, because he had an appointment there with a Mr. Tooley. Until then I hadn't visited Edwards because they specialize in voyages, travel, and the military—areas that I'm not interested in—but Ole convinced me to join him there. So while he went upstairs to see Mr. Tooley, I went downstairs to the basement where the art, architecture, and literature books were kept, and I found something marvelous there. Edwards had just bought the collection of the late Eric Newton, who was the art critic of the *Manchester Guardian* and the author of several books on art. They had sold the books and periodicals on ancient and Renaissance art and were eager to sell those on modern art and architecture—just up my alley. I bought the collection en bloc, and then treated Ole to a splendid lunch. He had taught me something that I have never forgotten: to make myself available to all kinds of opportunities by not shutting myself off from the possibilities that may come my way.

IS THE PRICE RIGHT?

I've put a lot of stuff about establishing prices for out-of-print books in Chapter 6, because that chapter deals with auctions, where there are no set prices and you need all the help you can get. But if you're not sure whether a dealer's prices are fair, you might want to read those sections now (pages 75–80).

Pricing second-hand, antiquarian, and out-of-print books is different from pricing new books. In new books, the publisher's price is usually printed on the inner flap of the dustjacket, and most dealers sell the book at the marked price or, if it is a discount store, at 10 percent to 20 percent below the marked price. (Publishers usually allow bookstores a 40-percent markup on hardcover trade—that is, non-text—books, so if volume is high enough and overhead low enough, discount booksellers can still make a profit.) While a book is still in print—still available from the publisher— a good second-hand copy may sell for anywhere from 25 percent to 50 percent below the listed price, again depending on the dealer. But the price of out-of-print books is something else. Out-of-print books are priced according to supply and demand factors. If the book is scarce and in demand, it may be selling for two or three times the publisher's price, or more. If the book is more common, the price may be lower than when it was originally published.

Most dealers want to be competitive and try to sell their books at what they feel are fair prices. They price their out-of-print books very carefully. They check the records of what each book brought at auction over the last five to ten years; they compare their price with the prices of their competitors; and they take into consideration the physical condition of the volume and what they paid for it. With all these considerations in mind, they arrive at a price. Still, prices vary from shop to shop. That is one reason for browsing in many shops—to do comparison shopping. Compare the price against the prices of other copies of the same book, the availability of the title, the condition of the book, and the strength of your desire for it. If you feel that the price is fair, then buy the book with pleasure. If you don't feel that the price is fair, don't buy it. Perhaps later you will reconsider, but that is useless hindsight if the book is no longer available.

Always keep in mind that pleasure is a difficult thing to measure in dollars and cents. If a book is beautiful to you and you feel that it belongs in your collection, then it is by all means a bargain, for you have acquired and made part of you something that will give you pleasure for a long time to come.

If you find later that the price you paid was too high in terms of what other dealers are charging, don't worry about that either. In the years that I have been buying and selling books, prices have caught up to and surpassed my biggest boo-boos. The pleasure I received also increased with time, and that was worth even more than the increase in price.

INSTALLMENT BUYING, CREDIT, AND DISCOUNTS

At times you may come upon an item that is expensive for you, and yet you wish to buy it because the price is fair for that item, or it is something unusual that you may have trouble finding again. What to do? Talk to the dealer and ask him or her if it is possible to buy the item on the installment plan—that is, to pay it off in two or three installments. This is, of course, entirely at the discretion of the dealer. If you are a new customer, or if the amount is large, he or she may want the item to remain in his or her possession until it's totally paid for. It is also reasonable for the dealer to charge you a monthly interest on the unpaid balance, say 1 or 1-1/2 percent per month, which is the interest rate that most department stores and credit cards charge. Get a receipt for each payment you make, and be careful; make sure that the payment schedule you have agreed on is one that you can meet without a strain on your resources.

If you see an item that you can afford but don't have a check or enough cash with you to pay for it immediately, again consult the dealer. Most will allow you to leave a deposit; make sure to get a receipt. Agree to a time (usually within thirty days) to pay off the balance.

Some dealers accept credit cards. Most dealers accept checks. If you are a new customer, they may want to hold the book until your check clears; or, if the book is expensive, they may want a certified check, cashier's check, or money order. This means extra effort and expense on your part, but the future goodwill may be well worth it.

Keep in mind that the dealer is expecting to receive the price marked. If you want a book that you feel is too expensive for you, you may ask the dealer if he or she can do anything about the price. Sometimes it works, other times it doesn't. The dealer may give you a slight discount, depending on the amount of books you are planning to buy, or on the way you ask for it; the psychological factor is extremely important. If the dealer refuses to give you a discount, you shouldn't be upset or disturbed any more than if you refuse to pay the dealer's price. If you find a price too high, do as dealers do; pass the item by, understanding that you can't buy everything and that some items are going to be too expensive.

Bookdealers do customarily get a 10 percent trade discount from other bookdealers. This is an advantage. But then, dealers have the disadvantage of having to mark up the price for resale, which a private collector doesn't have to do; unless, of course, you are buying the book for the express purpose of reselling it as a profit—and then you are really a dealer in disguise.

THE DEALERS' ASSOCIATION AND A UNIQUE SHOP

You'll find that as you get to know the dealers you'll like them better, and they'll be more interested in helping you. I try to get to know my colleagues in person so that by the time I visit their shops I am more than a name on a card or a listing in a directory. This is one reason that dealers participate in or attend book fairs and belong to professional associations, and one reason that I belong to the Antiquarian Booksellers Association of America, Inc. (ABAA), which is affiliated with the International League of Antiquarian Booksellers (ILAB).

The ABAA's aims include promoting the highest standards of bookselling; furthering good relationships between its members and the book-buying public; and upholding the status of the antiquarian book trade. Booksellers are admitted to membership on the recommendation of other booksellers and after three years of experience in the antiquarian book trade. If a dealer isn't a member of the ABAA, it doesn't necessarily mean that he or she doesn't meet the membership requirements; many dealers aren't joiners and prefer to remain independent of associations.

Some ABAA members participate in a unique shop in New York City called the Antiquarian Booksellers Center. This is a cooperative bookstore, offering selections for sale from the stock of seventy-six booksellers—a cross-section of books, autographs, maps, and prints, ranging from Americana to zoology, from incunabula to modern first editions. The variety of its stock is reflected in the variety of its prices, which range from $5 to $5,000.

The shop is located at 50 Rockefeller Plaza in the Associated Press Building of Rockefeller Center. (Rockefeller Plaza is parallel to and one-half block west of Fifth Avenue at 50th Street.) It's managed by a charming and knowledgeable lady, Edith Wells, who can help you see what is available at the shop and put you in touch with other dealers who are members of the ABAA and who might be of help to you with your collecting problems. When you are in New York, you must visit this special shop, meet Miss Wells, view the books on display, pick up the catalogues published by shop members, and spend a few pleasant hours in this book oasis amidst the hustle and bustle of midtown Manhattan. Or, if you cannot make it in person, write to Miss Wells and ask her to put you in touch with the participating dealers who specialize in your area. Also ask her for the newsletter that the center publishes from time to time.

An added attraction is that the shop shares its space with ABAA headquarters, presided over by Janice Farina, ABAA's capable executive secretary. Here you can see a display of catalogues of many ABAA members and pick up the map I told you about that shows where the New York dealers are located.

BUYING IN EUROPEAN SHOPS

This subject is worthy of a whole book; perhaps my next book will be devoted to my buying experiences abroad. If you've ever bought anything in a European shop, you'll appreciate how important it is to understand the national psychology of buying and selling.

In Great Britain and Ireland there is hardly a problem. The same holds true for the Scandinavian countries and Holland, Luxembourg, West Germany, and Switzerland, where most antiquarian bookdealers understand English, or members of their staffs do. The problems start in the Latin countries. France, and especially Paris, is a difficult place to buy books in unless you have a speaking knowledge of the language. Also in France, unless you are known or have written ahead, you will most likely be received as though you were invisible. You will hardly be noticed. If you should find something, you will have to take it with you rather than have it sent, unless you have bought a whole caseful of books. The French, for the most part, hate to mail things and will charge you in advance for the postage, packing, registration, and so on, which adds up to a tidy sum these days. As far as prices go, you can try to bargain. At times it works. They will be taken off balance and in sheer amazement may break down and grant you a discount—if they like you. The Belgians are easier than the French, since they don't insist that you speak French. They will try to meet you halfway in English, Flemish, or even German. Here, too, one can try to bargain, but it isn't always successful.

Italy, Spain, and Portugal are the countries where bargaining is a daily pastime. Italy especially. I remember once in Bologna I spent the entire morning trying to buy a small collection of futurist manifestos. The price the dealer asked was really high. I insisted that I wasn't going to pay that much. We haggled— I in my poor French and worse Italian—for two hours. By noon I'd had enough. "*Basta* (enough)," I said, and walked out. The dealer followed me down the two flights of stairs and into the street, talking faster than ever. Finally, without warning, he reached out for my hand and shook it violently. "*Daccordo* (okay)," he smiled, and immediately whisked me off to the nearest *caffè* for an *aperitivo*. He had agreed to my offer, but he was in such good spirits, so happy. (I heard from other dealers later that I had made his day.) It was a glorious morning for him, spent in the ancient art of bargaining. He even treated me to lunch. In Spain and Portugal, the art of bargaining is less developed, but its presence is felt.

The Italian post is not very good, so if you buy books in Rome, go to Vatican City and use the post office there. If you buy books in northern Italy, go to Switzerland, from where many Italian dealers mail their parcels. For more information about mailing books, see Chapter 5.

Your attitude in buying from European shops should be essentially the same as your attitude here. You will need more patience and humor to enjoy the experience, but if you come prepared it can really be fun. I see it as a game, and I enjoy playing it. In the morning before I leave my hotel, I warm up, reviewing the "national psychology" in my mind and trying to anticipate what the main events of the day will be. Then—ready, set, go!

CHAPTER 5

Buying by Mail

Buying by mail can be a wonderful means of enlarging your collection and learning about prices and the material as well. The majority of antiquarian booksellers mail out catalogues, lists, or letters offering items for sale. Most of these dealers will also search for titles which you need once they know your desiderata, and will let you know by mail when they find them. They may also offer you, by mail, items that they have recently purchased or have been offered that fall into your field of collecting. Most of my business is conducted by mail—I buy over 50 percent of my stock through the mail and sell over 90 percent of my stock by mail—and I for one can tell you that doing business by mail can be convenient, reliable, and at times most rewarding.

Here are some tips to make your buying by mail successful.

CATALOGUES

The most common form of buying by mail, and the one that offers the most varied choice, is buying from catalogues. Book catalogues come in all shapes and sizes, from the simplest mimeographed one- or two-page offering (usually called a list) to the most elaborate hundred-page-or-more bound catalogue, beautifully printed on coated stock with extensive descriptions and illustrations of the items offered for sale. Catalogues that also contain an introduction explaining the collection, an index, and a listing of references cited are called reference catalogues, since many collectors and librarians keep them for years and use them as a source of information about their collections and as a reference for pricing.

If the catalogue is an elaborate one, there may be a charge for it. I now charge $12 a year for a subscription to the year's four or five catalogues, because the cost of producing, printing, and mailing them is so high that I cannot afford to send them to everyone free of charge. Most other dealers do the same. Some dealers, including myself, refund the price of the catalogue from any item purchased from it. I think catalogues are worth paying for in terms of the amount of information you get out of them, as well as the opportunity to buy the items; in fact, if you see that a dealer regularly issues catalogues that are essential to you and your collection, I would pay extra to have that dealer's catalogues sent by first-class mail. In the long run the items you will be able to buy and the knowledge you pick up will more than pay for the subscription.

Most catalogues fall somewhere in between the extremes of the simple list and the elaborate reference tool. And all catalogues have the same primary purpose—to sell the dealer's stock that is offered therein. To make it easy for customers to order, catalogues usually contain the following information, although the order may vary. There are the name, address, and telephone number of the dealer. There is the date, often including the season or month as well as the year. There is a number indicating that this listing is one in a series issued by the firm. If the dealer does business outside of the United States, there may be a cable or telex word or number standing for the firm's name and address, and a special code word designating the particular catalogue. The code word will mean, "Please send the following items from your catalogue number so and so." This enables the overseas buyer to save on cable costs by using one code word rather than paying for the ten words otherwise needed to say the same thing.

Especially important to the buyer are the conditions of sale, which may state, for example, "All prices are net [that is, no discounts]. Postage, insurance, handling, and registration are extra." The conditions of sale may specify the cost of handling. They may state the tax (in mail-order buying, residents of the state must pay the state tax, while out-of-town buyers are exempt). They may say that for new customers payment must accompany the order unless two trade references are sent. In this section also, there should be a statement of condition—for example, "All books are complete and in good condition except where noted." There may be a money-back guarantee—that is, the books may be returned within a given period, usually a week to ten days after the customer receives them; if there is no such guarantee, you may prefer not to send your payment until after you have seen the books. Many catalogues will include an order form for you to use in ordering the items. If you do not include a check or money order with your order, then sign the order form; this legally confirms your order.

HOW TO ORDER

To make sure you get the items you want from a catalogue, it's advisable to phone—even long-distance—or cable for them before someone else does. Remember, good items are sold right away, and most likely the dealer has only one copy. The trade will pounce on it before you have a chance unless you act fast, and I mean *fast*. The day you receive the catalogue, read it, or at least the section that is of most interest to you, and pick up that phone and call in the order. This will temporarily reserve the books for you.

When you hang up, write out the order and send it to the dealer immediately—by airmail if the firm is overseas. It is essential to confirm calls and cables in writing. For example, if you have phoned in your order, you might write it out as follows:

Date

Bookseller's name
Address

Dear ———— [name of firm or owner/manager]:

Today I telephoned the following order, which I wish to confirm;
I ordered items nos. so and so from your catalogue no. such and such.

Please send an invoice in duplicate by mail [airmail, if overseas].

> Sincerely yours,
> Signature
> And your name and address, if they are
> not on your letterhead

If you cabled your order, confirm it as follows:

Date

Bookseller's Name
Address

Dear ————:

Today I have sent the following night letter [cheaper than a cable]:
STARS [or whatever the code word is] nos. 27, 154, 678.

Please send an invoice in duplicate by [air] mail; or an [air] mail report,
if the items were sold previous to my order.

> Sincerely yours,
> Signature
> Name and address

Now let's go over the reasons for these forms. You ask for two
copies of the invoice so that you'll have one for your records and
another to send back to the firm with your check. This is especially
important for overseas orders, since you may be sending a bank
draft that will not have your name on its face.

You ask for an immediate report on whether you have been
successful in your purchases because the same items may appear

in another catalogue you receive in the next days, and here you are not knowing whether you have already bought the item.

You include your name and address so the dealer will know to whom to send the items. It's surprising how many people forget to include this essential information. Be sure to include it in your cables, too. I regularly receive cables from a museum in London that include the name of the person ordering, but never the name of the institution. This, I assume, saves the institution time—and its name is on the follow-up letter. Nevertheless, I always call ITT and ask them to trace the sender; and usually within twenty-four hours they inform me. The dealer feels reassured when he or she knows who is ordering the items.

A letter of confirmation is important to you because mistakes may be made in transcribing oral or cabled instructions; and because your carbon or photocopy (and *always* keep a copy of your order) is important for your records. It is important to the dealer for several reasons. The first is that one is never sure about telephone calls until one receives a written confirmation, since there are people who call in and never follow up. The second is that if books are lost in the mail, the insurance company (if the dealer has one) will most certainly want to see a written purchase order before it pays off, and if there isn't one, then it's tough going on the claimant. The third reason is that dealers try to be fair when orders come in, filling the first request in writing for the given item. If you have phoned your order and you do not follow it up quickly with a letter or postcard, then the first written order the dealer receives will be the one to get the book; the dealer will not hold the item for more than a few days pending receipt of your written order.

HOPING FOR A DISCOUNT

If, in looking through a catalogue, you see a book that you want but you feel that the price is beyond what you wish to pay, you may write to the dealer and discreetly ask for a discount:

Date

Dear Bookdealer:

I saw on your recent catalogue [or list] no. ————, an item, no. blah blah, that I really want. However, the price is more than I can afford at the present time. If you do not sell the book in the near future, would you consider reoffering it to me at a somewhat lower price?

Sincerely yours,
Signature
Name
Address

This letter wouldn't cause any kind of ill feelings and might even get a favorable reply; but don't ever expect more than a 10 percent discount.

BUYING ON APPROVAL

You may prefer to see a book before you order it, particularly if you are not familiar with it. The best way to do this, if the dealer is in your city, is to make an appointment to go up and look at the book on the dealer's premises. If the firm is out of town and you cannot find a copy of the book in the library to' inspect, you can ask the dealer to send the book to you on approval.

"On approval" means you would like to see the book before you commit yourself to an outright purchase. It also implies that you are willing to pay the postage and insurance both ways— from the dealer to you and back to the dealer—and to make your decision within a set time. Usually the time is seven to ten days, after which you are obliged to keep and pay for the item. (The time the book is out of the dealer's hands may be much longer, for the mail is notoriously slow, and it may take three to four weeks for a parcel to travel coast to coast.) In sum, the procedure is similar to that used by the book clubs that send you a book for inspection—you may keep the book free for a few days, after which you are liable for it.

Many dealers will not send a book on approval when they have just mailed out a new catalogue, because they hope that the item will be sold to a client who knows the book and wants it outright. If the book hasn't been sold within thirty or forty-five days after the catalogue was mailed out, then the dealer may send it to you on approval. Please keep in mind that there is a risk in sending books on approval; they may be lost or damaged in the process, making it impossible, or at least more difficult, to sell them at a later date. If the dealer refuses to send you a book on approval, he or she is within his or her rights.

The dealer also has the right to send on approval parcels by certified mail or United Parcel Service so that he or she can have an exact record of the arrival time. You are obliged to pay for these extras. It should be stated in either your letter requesting the on-approval item or in the dealer's reply how the book will be sent; if the conditions are in the dealer's letter, you should acknowledge them in your answer.

If you send an on-approval book back, be sure to get a post office slip showing the date of mailing, so you have proof that it was mailed within the required period. This is especially important because book rate moves as fourth-class mail, and first, second, and third classes take precedence. Nevertheless, you should use book rate because it is the cheapest rate and is specially designed for books and printed matter. (Currently, book rate is 36¢ for the first pound; it increases 14¢ with each successive pound or fraction of a pound. The average octavo volume weighs about four pounds with packing.) Pack the book in a padded book bag—you can get one at a stationery store. Or you can reuse the wrapping the dealer sent the book in. If you do reuse this old carton or bag, make sure that it is reinforced in the spots that may have been torn or damaged when you opened the parcel. You can use string and waterproof plastic tape. Paste over all markings

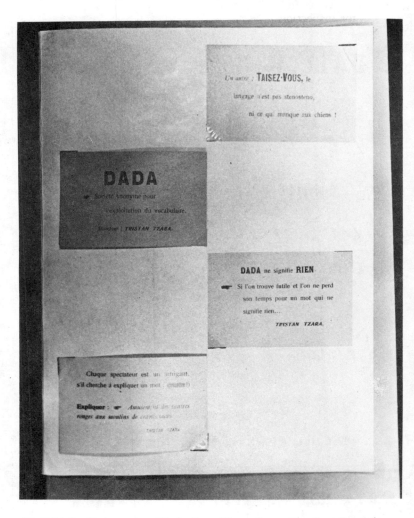

PLATE 1. Ephemera. Dada "papillons," small colored stickers with text by Tristan Tzara. *Photo by Michael Abramson.*

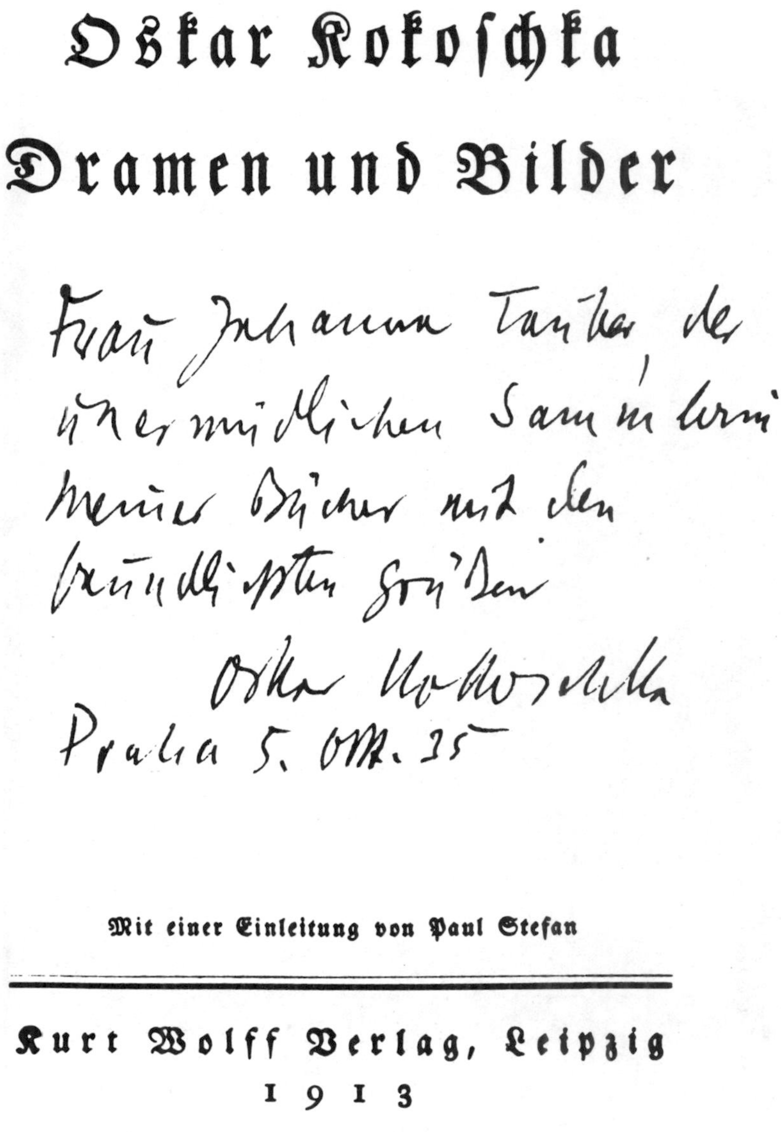

Oskar Kokoschka
Dramen und Bilder

[handwritten dedication]
Frau Johanna Tauber, der
unermüdlichen Sammlerin
meiner Bücher mit den
freundlichsten Grüßen

Oskar Kokoschka
Praha 5. OKT. 35

Mit einer Einleitung von Paul Stefan

Kurt Wolff Verlag, Leipzig
1913

PLATE 2. A handwritten dedication by the author adds value to a
book. This is the title page of Kokoschka's *Dramen und Bilder*,
signed, dated, and inscribed by Kokoschka to Frau Johanne
Tauber.

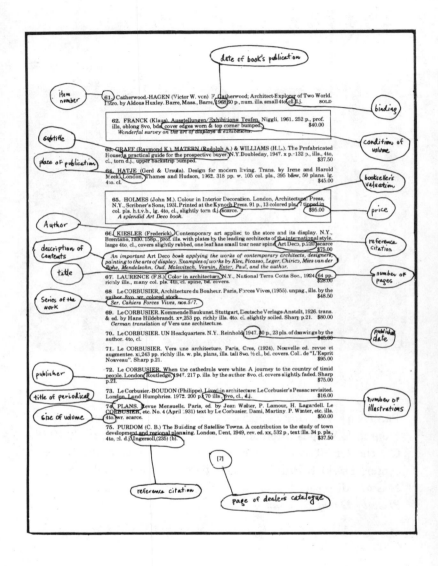

PLATE 3. Sample page from my Catalogue no. 52, explaining the terminology and abbreviations.

PLATE 4. The famous auction of a Gutenberg Bible at Christie, Manson & Woods International Inc., New York, April 7, 1978. On the left Robert Seaver, salesclerk, helps spot the bidders; center, David Bathurst, president, is auctioneer; right, Stephen Massey, director, books and manuscripts, notes the final bids. *Photo by David B. Ryan.*

PLATE 5. The quiet moment before a book fair is opened to the public. My booth; all the books, periodicals, posters, and ephemera were for sale.

PLATE 6. At a fair, the excitement touches the exhibitors as well as the visitors. This is the 14th New York International Book Fair at the Plaza Hotel, April 1978, and there I am, walking toward the camera. *Photo by Showcraft International, Inc.*

PLATE 7. A slipcase that is enclosed on all but one side creates a partial vacuum, causing the book to stick when removed, and eventually destroying the backstrip. *Photo by Michael Abramson.*

PLATE 8. The clam shell box, which has an attached cover, is the best type of box for books and periodicals. *Photo by Michael Abramson.*

PLATE 9. A glass-fronted bookcase provides maximum protection for books. *Photo by Michael Abramson.*

PLATE 10. This volume was kept on the lowest shelf of an open bookcase; notice the mop splatters on the cover. *Photo by Michael Abramson.*

with tape, or cross them out with a marking pen. Make sure your address is on the parcel.

Always include a note explaining the reasons for returning the item; if you have already sent the dealer a letter about it, enclose a copy of that letter.

INSPECTING YOUR PURCHASE

At times you may have to return a book that you have purchased outright. This can happen if, upon inspection, the book turns out not to be what it was supposed to be.

You will, of course, have kept the catalogue you ordered from—if not the entire booklet, then at least those pages that describe the items you have ordered—plus a copy of your letter ordering the books. When the parcel arrives, compare each book in it with its description in the catalogue. If they jibe, okay—you can now discard the catalogue page, if you don't need it for future reference. If they do not jibe, keep the description and write to the dealer, informing him or her of the discrepancy.

A book's defects, if any, may be hard to describe exactly, but the dealer should have mentioned the most obvious ones: for example, if the hinge (the place where the spine and inside covers of the book come together) is loose, or the binding is worn or marked, or the book is incomplete (that is, pages are missing). If the dealer didn't mention such defects, you have cause for complaint. You may wish to complain, too, if the date, publisher, or edition are different than listed; or if the dealer has stated that the item is in good condition, but your definition of "good" differs from the dealer's.

In any such cases, you have two choices. You can return the book with a note stating that the condition is such that you feel the item isn't as described and you are returning it for a refund; this approach will cost you return postage and insurance. (When returning a book, always have it insured at the post office and keep the receipt, for if it is lost on the way back you are responsible for it.) Or, if you do not agree with the dealer's assessment but you still want to keep the book, you can write to the dealer, explain why you disagree with him or her, and ask that he or she reduce the price. When a difference in opinion as to the condition of a book is involved, a fair reduction is usually 10 percent. If the matter is more serious than 10 percent would cover, then I suggest that you return the book.

It is important for you to be happy with your purchases. Dealers, too, want their customers to be happy. For the dealer, a good relationship and the probability of future sales, plural, are more important than just one sale followed by bad feelings. But you must make your complaint known to the dealer immediately. Other customers may want to buy the book as is, and the dealer can't sell it to them while he or she still thinks that it has been sold to you.

CATALOGUE FRINGE BENEFITS

As I said before, catalogues are good reference tools even if you don't want to buy any of the items in them immediately. They are also good sources of information about dealers. If you get a catalogue from a dealer whom you haven't done business with yet, but who seems to have items in your area, you can write to him or her and ask to be put on the mailing list. You can also send in a want list and ask that if these titles become available they should be offered to you. But please be serious about this request. If the dealer does offer you items in the future, and you aren't interested because you already have the items or something, please reply, thank the dealer for his or her efforts, and mention why you don't need those books.

In short, a catalogue can lead to the beginning of a good relationship between you and the dealer. As in all good relationships, there must be mutual trust and honesty. If one party takes unfair advantage of the partnership, then the other will soon find out and the special relationship will be broken.

BUYING FROM OVERSEAS CATALOGUES

Buying from foreign catalogues is essentially the same as buying from American ones, but there are a few safeguards you should observe. Be especially aware of the currency or exchange rates. As I write this, the Canadian dollar is worth $85\frac{1}{2}$¢ to the American dollar, and the British pound is worth $1.95. You can find the exact daily rate of all the major world currencies in the business section of most large city newspapers and in the financial section of the *Wall Street Journal.* They are printed in a box showing their worth against the U.S. dollar. Or phone your bank for the daily exchange rates.

The important thing to remember when ordering from abroad is that the exchange rate on the day you send in your order may have changed by the time you receive the book. So if the dollar drops, in effect you will be paying more than you had figured when you ordered the item. In 1978, I saw the Swiss franc strengthen by 16 percent against the dollar in three months, which meant that the books I ordered from Switzerland in June for $100 cost me $116 in September. (Three months is the average time span given for an overseas purchase on credit, since the book takes anywhere from six to eight weeks to reach New York, and then another couple of weeks to reach you if you are living in the western part of the United States.) Of course, if the dollar goes up, you will come out better than you had expected.

Receiving catalogues from abroad. Write to the foreign dealers who specialize in your area and ask to be put on their mailing lists. Remember that if you receive a British or European catalogue by ordinary boat post, the likelihood that the item you are interested in is still available when you get the catalogue is very remote. For this reason, it is best to receive all catalogues from abroad by airmail, even if this means paying the airmail costs in advance.

Even if you do receive the catalogues by airmail, it may be too late. In 1965 I received a list from a French dealer near the German border. There was a item in it that I wanted badly—a run of the *Poster*, an English periodical that is one of the best for posters. I couldn't reach the dealer by phone, so I sent him a cable. I never heard from him about it—a very common procedure with most European and even English dealers; if you do not request an airmail reply informing you that you were unsuccessful, you may never know whether you got the book—so I assumed that the item had been sold. A few months later I visited a dealer in Stuttgart, and lo and behold, there on his shelf was the same run of the *Poster*. I knew it was the same run because the numbers he had were identical, and such exact duplication is almost impossible. I asked the dealer if he had bought the run from our French associate, and he said yes. I bought the run from the Stuttgart dealer—at one-and-a-half times the price the French dealer had asked!

I don't waste my time ordering from a catalogue that hasn't been received by air. I will read it later, when time permits, just to keep up with the prices and see if there are items of interest, but I really don't expect to get anything if the catalogue has been sent by regular mail.

Understanding the language. Before ordering from a foreign catalogue, make sure you understand the terminology used to describe the book; ignorance is not considered an acceptable excuse for returning a book. With the British, Canadian, Australian, New Zealand, etc., dealers, there's no problem; the entire English-speaking book world uses the terminology originally developed in the British book trade. We follow the same descriptive bibliographies, cataloguing procedures, abbreviations, and terms for book sizes, although the British may be more exact (and note that they may give the size in centimeters). But if you receive catalogues from other countries, you should have some good English/foreign-language dictionaries around so that you can translate the terms used in the descriptions. Or you can buy, from the Antiquarian Booksellers' Association of America, the *Dictionary of the Antiquarian Book Trade*, edited by Menno Hertzberger. It costs $20. This work lists the technical terms used by English, Danish,

Dutch, French, German, Italian, Spanish, and Swedish antiquarian booksellers to describe the editions, conditions, virtues,
and faults of the items they offer for sale. There is a simple system
for cross-referencing from any one of the languages to any other.

You will find that in any language there are about thirty-six
or so words that are used over and over again in book descriptions.
These are key words, and you will soon get to know them if
foreign catalogues become your regular reading matter. Many
catalogues use abbreviations, too, and often the words these abbreviations stand for are listed on the inside front cover. But
before you can understand the abbreviations you will have to
know the words, so use your dictionary.

Overseas ordering. If you have received an airmail copy of a catalogue from abroad, have found an item you really need, have
computed the exchange rate, and still find the item attractive,
then telephone the dealer. It is easier than you think. First you
figure the time difference—five to six hours ahead of those of us
on Eastern Standard Time—and call at a time when the dealer
is likely to be in (not lunchtime, when in many European countries
businesses are closed altogether). You can dial direct to most large
English and European cities. If you are calling a small town or
you want to speak person-to-person, dial "0," ask for the overseas
operator, and give the country and the number listed in the
catalogue. When you get through, you can speak English—or,
if you know the language of the country, speak that.

If you feel inhibited about phoning, you can send a night letter,
which is an international cable limited to twenty-one words,
including the name, street address, city (the country is free), text,
and signature. Most European and British dealers have a cable
address, so use that to save words, but be sure to put in the
country as well. If there is a code word for the catalogue, use
that, too. It stands for "Please send the following books from
Catalogue so-and-so." Always give your name at the end so the
dealer can identify the cable.

A night letter to all European countries except Great Britain costs $2.92; to Great Britain, the cost is $2.50. Each extra word is 13¼¢ (11½¢ to Great Britain). A regular cable ("full letter") costs 26½¢ per word. ITT and Western Union both provide these cable services.

Always confirm your phone or cable order in writing the same day. To do this, you can use an aerogramme, which can be purchased at the post office for 22¢. It is an airletter consisting of one sheet which is folded twice to form an envelope and sealed at the ends and at the top. Or if you are ordering only one or two numbers, you can send a postcard by airmail, which costs only 21¢. Get airmail stickers at the post office—they are free— and place them on the lower left-hand corner of the card. A regular airmail letter will cost you 32¢ for the first half-ounce. Use airmail stationery and envelopes; they are lighter in weight than the ordinary ones. If you don't have airmail stationery, ordinary stationery will do provided you mark "airmail" on both sides of the envelope, or use the airmail stickers on both front and back.

Or use the order form which most European dealers enclose with the catalogue. Usually, the name of the country isn't marked on it, so type or write it in. Sign your name, and send it off.

Whichever way you choose, when ordering the items you want specify the item number as listed and the first word of the description (usually the author's name or book title), which is usually printed in the catalogue in bold type. If there are two or more items with the same first word, list the second word, too, so that there is no doubt as to the item you want. It takes a few seconds longer, but it can avoid much trouble and expense later on. The clearer and more precise you are, the less possibility there is for mistakes or misunderstanding.

Place the catalogue and your carbon copy of the order in an alphabetical file folder under the dealer's name until the books arrive. Then you will be able to compare the description, price, and condition with the actual book. If there are discrepancies, you will be within your rights to return the book or ask for a reduction in price.

Shipping and customs. You are responsible for the postage, registration or insurance, and handling (packing) costs of the books you order. Depending on the amount of books you purchase, on overseas purchases these charges can add 10 percent to the cost if the book is $50 or more; under $50, the relative percentage is usually greater.

To save money, always, *always* specify in your order how the books are to be sent. The usual cheapest way is by registered boat post. The books will take from six to ten weeks to arrive from Europe, depending on the proximity of the country and the efficiency of its post. Once the books arrive in the United States, they are moved as "certified mail." You have to sign for the parcel, so make sure someone is there to sign for it; otherwise, it goes back to the post office and you will have to make an extra trip to pick it up.

If you are ordering only one or two books and they are expensive, it may pay to have them sent by insured air freight. That's much faster, and the rates aren't too much higher. Your dealer can inform you of the difference if you request it in your order letter or confirmation; then you can decide if the difference between surface mail and air is worth your while.

If you do not specify the manner of the shipment, dealers are within their rights to send it the most convenient way for them, which may be the costliest way for you. They can have the books packed, trucked, and forwarded to a customs broker who will send the books to another broker in the States, and you will be responsible for all the charges, including the freight, storage, and brokers' fees here and abroad. This can be very expensive—it could cost you over $100 just for the carriage. I have had this happen to me a few times even though I have specified how the books were to be sent, because my instructions weren't followed.

It is vital that you keep a carbon copy of your original order so that you have proof of your instructions. In a case where your instructions have not been followed, you may refuse acceptance of the charges and of the books. The books are then returned to the seller, who has to absorb the charges. But I do not recommend that you do this, since this will be your last dealing with the dealer. Also, you may want the books very badly, and returning them is not the most satisfying way of getting out of the mess. What I have done in a case like this is to telephone the dealer, inform him or her of the situation, and say that unless he or she pays the charges or deducts them from the cost of the books—assuming the books are worth more than the other costs—I will not accept them. Act very quickly, because books that are forwarded from broker to broker or that end up in customs are subject to storage charges after ten days or so, on top of all the other charges.

Speaking of customs, you should know that second-hand books are not subject to duty; but if the cost is over $250, they may have to be cleared, which means you have to send a copy of the invoice and fill out a form. (That's one reason for asking the dealer for a duplicate invoice; customs may ask for the original copy. If they do, make still another copy for your records, because one copy has to go back to the dealer with your payment.) If the books are in a foreign language, mention this fact when clearing them—foreign-language books seem to clear customs faster than English ones. In most cases, after you have complied with these rules the books will be delivered to you by mail.

One way to avoid all this red tape is to tell the dealer when you order that if the amount is more than $250, he or she is to make several shipments out of the lot, breaking the shipments up in such a way that no one shipment is over $250 (assuming, of course, that no single book costs over $250). Most foreign dealers know the rules and will automatically comply, but it is always wise to mention it in your order or confirmation letter.

You may have to pay a little more for the packing and postage, but believe me, it is well worth it compared to having the shipment end up in customs and the hassle of clearing the books.

Paying for foreign purchases. Usually payment is due on receipt of the books. However, many European dealers will not send a book abroad unless the customer is known to them, has established a credit line, and is on good terms with them. So if you are a new customer, the bookseller may require prepayment.

Regardless of whether you pay before or after you receive the book, keep in mind that most European dealers want payment in their own currency, especially when the American dollar is weak. If you are billed in dollars then you can pay in dollars, by sending a personal check or money order (bank or post office). But if you are billed in a foreign currency, you must pay in that currency. The bank or post office will charge you a fraction of a percent higher for the foreign currency than the official exchange rate as quoted in the newspapers.

You can pay in a foreign currency by buying an international money order at the post office. The fees are 90¢ for amounts from 1¢ to $10; $1.10 for $10.01 to $50; and $1.40 for $50.01 to $300. If the amount you have to pay is more than $300, you can send two or more money orders.

Another method, which costs slightly more on amounts over $200 but saves you waiting in the post office and also takes less time to reach the recipient, is to have your bank send a draft in the foreign currency to a bank in the city where the dealer is located. Most large commericial banks have branches or correspondent banks in capitals or principal cities abroad. They can send the draft directly to that bank, and the dealer can either pick it up there or have it transferred to his or her own account. The bank will charge you 32¢ for the airmail notice sent to the correspondent bank. Or you can send the bank draft, with a copy of the invoice, directly to the dealer. Many foreign dealers prefer the latter practice; and I prefer it, too, because it gives me control over when and how the draft is sent.

Another alternative is available when the bookseller has a dollar account in an American bank, as many large international booksellers have. In this case, you can send the dollar equivalent of the order, with the invoice, directly to the dealer's bank in the United States. If you do this, be sure you send the correct amount; you can ask your bank, or the bookseller's, the exchange rate on the day you pay. Usually with such an account the check is made out to the order of the bank, so you must include a copy of the invoice, and the dealer's name and account number for proper crediting.

Whichever method you use, try to settle up your accounts with foreign dealers as soon as you receive the books—remember, the dealer has already waited for payment six to ten weeks while the books were in transit.

Shall I return? If, when you get the book, you find it differs from its description, you can write to the dealer and inform him or her that the book is not as described in the catalogue, and therefore you feel free to return it. Mention what the discrepancies are. Then pack the item as well as or better than when you received it. Ideally, you should have kept the wrapping so that you can return it in the same material it was sent in. Always send the book back by registered or insured mail, and keep the insurance or registration receipt from the post office for proof of mailing. You may deduct the cost of the postage and registration or insurance from the cost of any other items on the invoice; or, if you ordered only the one item, you may inform the dealer that he or she should credit you for the postage, etc., against your next purchase.

If the book isn't as described but you like it anyway, or returning the item isn't worth your time and expense, you can write to the dealer, tell him or her how you feel, and suggest a slight price reduction to offset the difference between your interpretation of the book's condition and the dealer's description. Most dealers would rather adjust the price than run the risk of return and the possibility of the book being lost or damaged on the way. As with American dealers, a fair reduction is usually about 10 percent; if you feel that doesn't cover it, return the book.

Foreign "on approvals." Whether you can see an item from abroad on approval is totally up to the bookseller. If the item is still available several weeks after the catalogue has been published, the dealer may agree to send it if you will prepay all charges. You shouldn't keep an on-approval item from abroad more than a day or so, and you should return it the same way it was sent— that is, if you got it by airmail, you should send it back by airmail; or, if the dealer specifies the manner in which it should be returned, then comply with the dealer's wishes.

All these matters should be made clear in your letter to the bookseller requesting the item on approval. Nothing should be left to chance. You should say something like this:

> I am interested in item number_____and would very much like to see it if you would be willing to send it to me on approval. I either will keep the item or, if I do not take it, I will return it within a day or two after receipt by registered post or airmail [let the dealer decide] as you wish. I will pay for the postage, handling, and insurance or registration both ways if the item is returned. I look forward to hearing from you on this matter and assure you that I will take all the necessary precautions and care in regard to this transaction.

Some dealers will not send books abroad on approval under any circumstances, and others will; so please respect the dealer's decision.

CHAPTER 6

Buying at Auction

Since the seventeenth century, auctions have been a marvelous place to buy as well as learn about books and other objects. In the last few years, with inflation taking its toll of the shrinking dollar, more collectors, booksellers, and libraries have been selling books and periodicals at auction. An auction is a fun event as well as serious business. Attending one in person is very exciting. To mingle with the pros, to participate in an event that is open-ended, to witness the tension of the bidding, and on occasion to see something knocked down for a record price is as thrilling as watching a thoroughbred race. And it can be just as dangerous financially.

To avoid "auction fever"—the spell of being sucked into a price battle between bidders—you have to prepare yourself very carefully.

START SMALL

For the beginner, the best way is to start by attending an auction sale that isn't exclusively devoted to books but does contain a section of books. A whole auction devoted to books, an auction that may take a whole day or even two days, can be a little overwhelming. So start with a small selection of books.

INSPECT THE BOOKS BEFORE THE AUCTION

Take a look at the books during the presale period, which usually extends from a few days before the actual auction until the day of the sale, or a few hours before the sale. If you've started small, you'll be able to view a manageable amount of books in a leisurely manner, inspecting those of interest to you, noting their condition, collating them to make sure that all the sections are present—that no plates or pages are missing or damaged—that the front and back flyleaves, the half-title page, and the title page are present if published. Note any markings or stains in books and periodicals. Check the condition of the page edges and test the binding. If the spine is cracked, the backstrip torn, or the hinges missing, the book will be worth less.

Is the book a first edition? Does it contain a handwritten dedication from the author, or does it come from the library of another famous person? If it does, it is an association copy, and therefore more valuable. Does it have a handwritten or autographed letter (an A.L.) enclosed? Are other significant documents included, such as a visiting card, a menu, extra plates, newspaper clippings or reviews? Is the book specially bound, or is the binding elaborate, perhaps leather, or tooled, or gilt-edged? All of these conditions are extras that enhance the book and make it more desirable—and also more expensive.

If the binding is other than the publisher's, the book will be worth more to some collectors. For other collectors, who insist on collecting books in the original binding without any alterations, a new binding would detract from a book's desirability. On the other hand, there is a group of collectors—the fine-binding bund, I call them—who buy books just for their bindings. Their interest is in the beauty, workmanship, and originality of the binding. Some of these collectors who buy rebound books like to have the original wrappers the volume was published in bound in. Remember, today the cost of binding is high and going higher because of increasing labor and material costs. If you have decided to collect books that are nicely bound, then add the cost of the binding to your auction price.

Often collectors of fine bindings are also interested in illustrated books that are published in a limited edition on fine paper and feature good illustrators or artists. Always pay close attention to these conditions, because a copy of a book in a limited edition is worth more than a copy in an ordinary edition. The colophon of a limited-edition book will state the number of copies printed, the kind of paper used, how many special copies were reserved for the author or artists, and whether the plates were destroyed after the run. The special copies will usually be numbered. They may carry a Roman numbering for, say, the first fifty or seventy-five examples. These copies may be printed on a better grade and quality paper and not be available for commercial sale but reserved for the collaborators and/or subscribers. They may be on Arches paper or vellum, they may be signed by the author and/or the artist, and they may even be numbered by hand. The early numbers may contain an original graphic that the later numbered copies or the ordinary edition will not have. These small differences are large when it comes to pricing; the more exclusive and elaborate an edition or run is, the more it is worth and the higher the price it will bring. Keep all these factors in mind as you go on to the next step in evaluating the books.

CHECK THE RECORDS

The next step is to check out individual books to see if they're still in print. I'm always amazed at auctions to find some books that are still in print bringing higher prices than the publisher's retail price simply because the bidders did not take the time to check out the title in *Books in Print* or because they got caught up in that old auction fever and went beyond their limits. *Books in Print*, published annually by the R.R. Bowker Company, lists every book in print in this country. It is available in most retail, second-hand, and antiquarian bookshops, and in libraries. Most booksellers are only too glad to check out a title or two for you; or, if there are many titles, you can do your own investigating. That's better anyway, because you can begin to learn prices in this simple fashion.

While you're looking through *Books in Print*, check to see if the title you're interested in is available in paperback. Today, with the enormous paperback market, it may well be; and in some cases this will affect the price. Not that you shouldn't buy the original edition if there's a reprint available—in fact, the original editions of most books are not affected by paperbacks. However, later hardcover editions may drop in value.

In any case, the paperback should provide you with a comparison with the edition offered at auction as well as a reference tool to the author's other works. If you are collecting an author, all the knowledge you can get about him or her—his or her works, editions, and works about the author—will contribute to your information and pleasure. I have always believed in buying, or at least reading, whatever was available in print on a given author, area, or subject; this approach provides an ambiance for the collector as well as a foothold into the specifics of the field of collecting.

At the library, *Books in Print* will be in the reference section along with some other important tools: the auction records. These are works that show what prices books have brought at auction. There are two important book-auction records. The first is *American Book Prices Current*, which contains over 29,000 entries from over 150 sales of books, manuscripts, maps, and broadsides sold at auction in the United States, Canada, and Europe. The series is published annually, but it covers auctions that took place over a year before. The second is the *British Book Auction Records*, a priced and annotated annual record of international book auctions. This is also published annually, but quarterly issues are now available on subscription, offering readers more timely information on auction prices.

When you use the auction records, always remember to note the prices for several years—going back, say, to 1970, when prices really took off. Add the prices for a given work over these years and divide by the number of years to get an average or median price.

Note the description of the entry in the records to see if it corresponds to the book in the auction you're going to attend. Remember the factors you noted when you inspected the books. If your book is damaged, it will be worth less than the one listed in the auction records (unless that one is damaged, too). If it's in a fine binding or has other extras, it will be worth more. The books you look up should correspond as closely as possible to the book in the auction.

After you have checked the auction records, check prices in dealers' catalogues, following the same procedure. If you can't get your hands on dealers' catalogues at the moment, try a work published by the Gale Research Company called *Bookman's Price Index*. This series includes over 400,000 listings for books and periodicals offered by the world's leading rare booksellers, specialist dealers, and out-of-print book people. Arranged alphabetically by author, each entry notes the author, title, place and date of publication, pagination or collation, condition, dealer's name and catalogue numbers, item numbers, year of catalogue's publication, and price of the item. Check out the last five or six years.

DECIDING HOW MUCH TO BID

Now you are ready to decide how much you will bid. You know the average price the book has brought at auction and what dealers charge for it. If the book you're going to bid on is a fine copy, in a limited edition, or specially bound, add 10 to 25 percent to the average price it has brought. If it is in poor condition, with a torn publisher's binding, deduct 10 to 25 percent. The final determinants of the price will be your experience and how much you want the book.

Write your prices in your auction catalogue in code. I suggest that you adopt a code at the very beginning of your collecting—it will come in handy for all sorts of things. At an auction, it will prevent the people sitting next to you from seeing what you are prepared to bid (you can never tell who will be sitting next to you at an auction).

A good code for collectors is a substitution code—a group of numbers or letters substituted for the Arabic numbers from 1–9 and zero. You can use your name, for example, if it contains ten different letters. Or you can adopt a word that is real, or make one up. Take the word "Jerusalimo," which fits exactly. The "J" is the designation for the number 1; the "e" for 2; "r" for 3; and so on through "o," which becomes zero. With a little time and practice, "Jerusalimo" will become second nature to you. This code will be useful at an auction; simply mark your price in code to the left of each item you're interested in, and the auctioneer's estimates to the right (unless the estimates are already printed at the end of each entry). Or save the right side for the prices the items reach during the sale; this will be a valuable guide the next time these books come up at auction.

PRICING BOOKS BY THE LOT

Sometimes instead of being sold individually, books at auction are grouped into lots. A lot contains anywhere from three items up. Sometimes the lots contain a random selection of books; sometimes they are grouped by author, artist, or subject.

The books in the lot are usually not of equal value, since one of the purposes of selling the books this way is to dispose of several less desirable books along with one or two good ones.

You can inspect and research lots the same way as you do individual books. When it comes to deciding the amount you want to bid for the lot, it's best to establish a price for the one or two important items and not to bid beyond the worth of these.

Most lots contain many books that are common, and unless you're just starting to collect, you may find that you already own many of the titles in the lot. If you can get the lot for no more than the value of the important books, then it's worth it; you can always trade or sell the duplicates and the titles you don't want later on.

Actually, it's the professional booksellers who benefit the most from buying in lots, because they are buying for stock and can more easily dispose of all the titles. If a bookseller outbids you for a lot, after the auction ask the dealer if he or she is willing to part with the title you are interested in. If it's not the same one the dealer was interested in, he or she may be willing to sell it to you on the spot. The price you offer the dealer should be at least equal to your maximum bid on the lot, and at most your highest bid plus 10 or 15 percent.

NOW GET READY FOR THE AUCTION

It's very important to be calm, relaxed, and in good spirits when you attend an auction. Otherwise you can't enjoy the game.

I always have a good breakfast if I am going to a morning sale. In the afternoon, a light lunch—fish or eggs or poultry, nothing heavy enough to put you to sleep. And never have one too many, because after you sober up you may hate yourself for bidding too high—you know that high feeling, "Oh, what the hell, a couple of dollars more won't kill me." Well, it may not kill you, but it is irresponsible bidding. Remember, the next time the item is up for sale your bid may have contributed to its rise in price, and it was because of your feeling high rather than its intrinsic worth. Your bid will appear in the auction records if it's an important auction, and you now know what that can mean in establishing the price of a book. Have one drink if you need it to relax, but leave that high feeling for when you've acquired the item at a good or fair price.

POSITION YOURSELF

In a small auction house, meet the auctioneer before the sale, tell him or her who you are, and give him or her your card or your name and address for identification. If you wish to remain unknown, say so, and ask that the auctioneer use your initials or give you a code name for the auctions. Better still, if remaining inconspicuous is so important, have another person execute your bids; this will keep your name out of the auction records.

Sit in a section that has a good view of the dais so that the auctioneer can see you and you can see and hear him or her. I prefer to sit on the left aisle so that I have only one person to my right and can write the prices freely; I'm left-handed. I remember being at an important European auction where the bidding was in four languages—French, German, English, and Italian. It was imperative that I hear what was going on. But before the auction I met a Dutch colleague, a French dealer, and an American collector and his agent. We all sat together, which was a mistake. The American couldn't keep quiet for a second, and I was trapped between him and the Dutch dealer, who kept asking me what the auctioneer was saying. I had to pretend I was going to the men's room to get away from them.

Another advantage to an aisle seat is that you can leave at will without disturbing the auction. I always leave when all the items I care about have been auctioned off. In fact, I time myself so that I arrive just before the lots I'm interested in appear. Usually there are two sessions to an auction, morning and afternoon. Try to attend only the session of interest to you. If you are interested in items in both sessions, ask the auctioneer during the preview when he or she expects to reach the items you are bidding for, and arrive ten minutes or so earlier; give yourself enough time to find a spot or seat and work yourself into the auction leisurely.

HOW TO BID

The most important thing to remember about bidding is this: *Never go beyond the limit which you yourself have set.* The price you have listed must be your limit for that book or lot of books. Say you have decided to bid $25 for a book. You have written the code number ES near the number of the lot. Bid until the price reaches ES—$25—and, if you are not the successful bidder, *drop out.* Do not succumb to auction fever.

Another rule is not to bid continuously for an item. Wait until the auctioneer is about to close the bidding, just before or during the warning period when he or she says, "Do I hear any other bids?" or "Fair warning," and then raise your hand.

Raising your hand is the best way to bid. In the beginning, don't try to use a signal that is prearranged with the auctioneer. In fact, in my opinion, never use one—it only confuses most auctioneers and leads to mix-ups in prices and bidding. There's a story about a book collector whose signal was blowing his nose; one day he went to an auction with a cold, and by the time it ended he had acquired a considerable collection of things he didn't want—all because he used his nose instead of his head. So leave the signals to the experts who wish to remain anonymous.

IN-BETWEEN BIDS

There may come a time during an auction when your limit falls between the last bid and the next one announced by the auctioneer. For example, if your limit is $250 and the price goes up by twenties—the last bid was $240 and the next is $260—you will be caught between the last bid and the next, which is $10 over your limit. What to do? You can speak up and say, "I bid $250"; and on rare occasions the auctioneer will recognize your bid. If no one else bids against you, you will have the item. The fact that you have voiced an in-between bid is important if you are bidding for someone else who has given you a limit that has fallen between the price levels established by the auction house, since it is now a matter of record that you executed the bid faithfully and diligently, a fact that is very important if you are a dealer bidding for a client.

If the auctioneer doesn't accept your in-between bid and insists on the established price level, you are caught in a small fix. Having gone this far to the limit, the matter is out of your hands; you are not the one who is going beyond the limit you yourself have set. In a case like this, if you are buying the item for yourself, you must decide quickly whether or not it is worth the extra amount. I always go to the next price if I am bidding for myself. If I am bidding for a client, then I make it known that should a case like this arise, I want the client's authorization to go to the next price level; in most cases I get this permission.

If the amount is smaller, below $100, then I stay within the limit and let the item go.

AFTER THE AUCTION

After the sale, pick up your books if you have the money with you. This will save you an extra trip. If you want the books sent, give the auctioneer your instructions. Larger auction houses have a separate billing department that will make out your bill and include the postage and handling charges.

When you get the books home, check them out again to make sure they're complete, and catalogue them before you shelve them or read them.

ATTENDING AUCTIONS BY PROXY

If you have trouble sticking to your limit at an auction, one way out is to give your bids to a friend, a relative, or a bookseller. If you select a friend or relative who is not directly involved, the person will adhere strictly to your limit. A dealer will stick to your limit too, but you must expect to pay him or her a commission of 10 percent. The dealer's entitled to it. For this commission, he or she will buy the item for you, pay the auctioneer, and be responsible for the item's delivery—and its completeness, if you have instructed him or her to inspect it prior to the sale. The dealer is entitled to charge you the carriage, postage, handling, insurance, state and city taxes if applicable, plus any other charges incurred with the sale (telegram, long distance calls, etc.). You are expected to settle the account immediately, since the dealer has laid out the money, the time, and the labor.

Another good reason for using a dealer is that there's an important auction that you can't attend in person. My recommendation is to select a dealer whom you know and trust, and who specializes in your type of material; or any dealer who is reputable and solicits auction commissions. Ask the dealer to examine the books carefully during the preview period and to note the condition; for unless the book is an especially valuable one, auction houses don't collate the material themselves. Ring the dealer up and inquire about the condition. After receiving this report, you are free to lower or raise your bid accordingly.

ATTENDING AUCTIONS BY MAIL

Since you don't have to be physically present at an auction to bid, you don't have to restrict yourself to local auctions. Most auction houses accept written bids. But be careful. Before bidding in a foreign auction read the conditions of sale very carefully. They are usually printed on the inside front cover of the auction catalogue. European auction houses usually have the conditions of sale printed in two or three languages; one of them is English. All property is usually sold "as is." The auction houses are not responsible for correctness of description, genuineness, provenance, attribution, authenticity, authorship, completeness—the latter is particularly important when purchasing periodicals or serials, an area that I know only too well and have had the most trouble with at auctions—and condition of the property.

Remember, too, that in European auctions there is a 10 to 15 percent charge to the buyer on each lot—plus an item charge, in Dutch auctions. Keep in mind that the auctioneer will charge the official rate of exchange for the day of the auction, if you bid in dollars, in addition to postage, insurance, packing, and bank charges. For all of these reasons, always—and I mean *always*—write out your bids; or, if you telephone or cable, then confirm these bids in writing, always keeping a copy for your records.

Always convert your bid into the local currency. And always specify in your letter exactly how you wish the books sent (see Chapter 5), and how you wish them packed. Most European auction houses will pack the books for you at a nominal charge. The larger British houses, though, have a tendency to pass them on to a freight forwarder and/or packer, and this adds considerably to the cost of the books. A few years ago, I bid on a few books at Sotheby, was successful, and asked the house to pack the books. The books were knocked down at £95. But Sotheby passed them on to a packer, who constructed a wooden case for them —totally unnecessary, since they could have been packed in two parcels and sent as printed matter. The packer sent the books to a trucking firm for pick-up and delivery to the boat, and the truckers, in turn, sent the paper (invoice, bill of lading, bill for packing) to their bank. Their bank added a commission and had the paper sent to my bank for collection. My bank added collection charges. To top the matter off, when the case arrived in New York the customs service took over and held it for clearance. I had to send the original invoice to my broker, who cleared the parcel for another $49 (there's no duty on second-hand books). After all the charges were totaled, the cost of handling was more than the £95 I had paid for the books.

Don't let this happen to you. Always specify that if you are successful in obtaining the books they are to be sent by the auction house and not by a packer, forwarder, or whatnot. If the house doesn't have a packing department, then have the books picked up by a friend (mention his or her name in your letter); or better still, place your bids with an agent. If neither of these courses is possible, state that the books are to be sent the cheapest way (printed matter); that they are not to be crated (unless you buy a huge amount of heavy books, in which case it may be cheaper to go by ocean freight); that if there are many books, they can still go by printed matter, if they are packed together in postal sacks.

Here's a sample of a written bid that contains all this information:

> Your name
> Your address
> Date

Auction House
Address
City, Country

Name, if you know it, or Dear Auctioneer:

Please bid for me in your forthcoming auction ———— [give auction sale number or code word, if any] on ———— [give the date, because some houses have frequent auctions and receive mail for a few sales at a time] on the following item(s):

No. 476 Goethe . . .   Limit DM 30.00

[List the number of the entry and the first word, which is usually printed in the catalogue in bold type. If you are bidding on other items by the same author or of the same description, list the second word as well. On the right-hand side, list your bid in local currency. Be sure to include the word "limit" before the currency sign.]

Please send the book(s) by the cheapest way, insured post, printed matter, in parcels. Please send a copy of the invoice by airmail.

[Most European auctioneers will send the invoice by airmail anyway, but you should still specify it, for you want to know as soon as possible if you were successful, or if you have to continue searching for the items.]

> Yours truly,
> Signature

Keep in mind that the bill will most likely be a pro forma one that requests prepayment for the merchandise and shipping and/or packing charges. If you didn't have someone buying the items for you, then this is the blind spot. You have prepaid the item and carriage, it is on its way, and the risk is now yours. If an agent has bought the books for you, he or she is responsible for them once they have been removed from the auctioneer's premises.

COMPLAINTS

If the condition of the book you receive is not the way it was described in the auction catalogue, you can make a claim. If the books have been damaged in transit, your claim is against the insurance company (see Chapter 5). But books that do not meet the conditions of sale are the responsibility of the auction house.

If you have any complaints, for United States auctions you have about fourteen days from the date of the auction to make a claim. Claims must be in writing and sent by registered mail, return receipt requested; otherwise they are considered to be waived and without validity. European houses have similar rules, but in most cases the claim period is extended to three weeks or a month or "upon receipt of merchandise" for overseas customers. If your claim is accepted, you will either be credited with the amount (a nice situation for the auction house, since it has the money and you must bid again in forthcoming auctions to absorb the credit), or you can insist on receiving a refund by check.

FINDING THE AUCTIONS

To learn where and when auctions are taking place, I recommend that you subscribe to the seasonal or yearly sales catalogues of the larger auction houses (Sotheby Parke Bernet, Christie's, Swann, etc.—see Appendix). For a little more money, these houses will also send you records of the final bids. Paste the price list into the catalogue, if the catalogue contains books in your area, and you will have an important reference tool.

Most of the larger auction houses have several categories of catalogues. You can subscribe to the one you're interested in. For example, I subscribe only to the modern book auctions at Sotheby in London. At smaller auction houses, you can subscribe to all the catalogues, since the book auctions are of a general nature. Some European book dealers are licensed to conduct auctions; if you're on these dealers' mailing lists, you will receive their auction catalogues as well.

The cost of a yearly subscription to a house's catalogues is anywhere from $30 down. It's cheaper to buy individual catalogues at the time of the auction; but I don't recommend it, because there usually isn't enough time before the auction to check out the items you're interested in.

Subscribe to American catalogues by first-class mail if the auction house isn't in your city, or if you're the type of person who waits till the last minute to decide to bid. If you can attend to the catalogue as soon as you receive it, then ordinary third-class mail will be good enough. European auction catalogues should be received by airmail so that you can read them carefully and make the necessary evaluations in time (if you are lucky) to write or cable the auctioneer with your bid.

Another way to find out about auctions—local ones—is through the newspapers. Especially in the Sunday papers, there are announcements of forthcoming sales. And then there are the small auctions that don't have catalogues. There are districts in every city that specialize in these—in New York City, Greenwich Village is the place.

IN SUM

To sum up, auctions are fun to attend and a good way to buy and sell books. The art of auction buying, like any other art, takes time to perfect. Start modestly. Know what you want and how much it is worth. Sit in a good location and in direct sight of the auctioneer. Bid only on items that are of interest to you. And—have fun.

CHAPTER 7

Other Ways to Buy and Otherwise Acquire Books

I've already talked about the major methods of buying out-of-print books—from antiquarian bookshops, from catalogues, and from auctions. But there are still other places where, if you are lucky, you can find good books for your collection.

PRIVATE COLLECTIONS

Sometimes private collectors want to sell either parts of their library or their entire collection. (You may want to, too, some day; more about that in Chapter 10.) When you become known as a collector—and a good way to do that is to get yourself listed in the *International Directory of Book Collectors* (see page 38)—you will most likely receive mail from other collectors as well as from societies and clubs. In a very short time, you will get to know some of the other collectors in your specialty areas. Make a list of the titles that you would like to acquire, and send them to those collectors, asking if they can offer you any of the titles either in exchange for another book or through direct purchase.

In your list, try to be as specific as possible. List all the information you have on the item—the author, title, place of publication, publisher, date, edition, and the state and condition that is acceptable to you. A listing such as "Mark Twain—all" or "Picasso, anything on" is too general for a collector, and most discouraging. Your replies will be proportionately higher as you are more specific, because the other collector will see right away that you are serious and knowledgeable.

In all fairness, you should state on the list, or the cover letter accompanying it, that you are sending this list to several private collectors. Then you can feel free to get the book from the lowest bidder, and the other collector can feel free not to answer your request if he or she so chooses. And always include a self-addressed stamped envelope so that the other collector can reply with the least possible loss of time and money.

Under these conditions, most collectors will reply—wouldn't you?—and even if they don't want to sell or exchange the books you need, you might enjoy corresponding with a person who has the same type of interests as you. The book world can, if you want it to, expand into a very lively world indeed; but it is up to you to make the first move.

TRADING

I have just mentioned that some collectors may want to exchange books rather than sell them. Booksellers may sometimes indulge in trading, too. It's fun. It's also a good way of mutually satisfying needs.

But you have to establish guidelines. First make certain that you no longer want the book. Then be sure that the book you are trading it for is of comparative value. If the book you want to trade is worth more than the other collector's, you should ask for and receive the extra value; he or she can throw in another book or two to make up the price. You be fair, too. State the facts. You should inform the other collector that the price you have set on the book is the fair market value. If you aren't sure of the fair market value, you can trade on a cost-plus basis; that is, what the item cost you, plus what you have spent in time (cataloguing) and materials—say a slipcase, a new binding, repairs, and/or insurance (if it is an expensive item). If you are trading with a bookseller, please remember that there is an understanding that the dealer will have to resell the book; so the book the dealer offers in exchange may be worth a little less than the one you offer him or her.

After awhile you will get a sense of the worth of your books. If you feel that it is a fair exchange and the other person agrees, swap books and feel good about the deal. If you cannot live with the arrangement, don't finalize it. It is better in the long run to hold your books a little longer than to feel resentful or unhappy at a later date. With time, you will be more secure in handling this type of transaction; doing it again and again is the best way to learn.

BUYING FROM ESTATES

The first thing my old boss Paul Gottschalk used to do in the mornings was read the obituaries in *The New York Times*. If he came across a name that rang a bell, or if the obituary mentioned that the person had had a library, was a member of the Grolier Club, or had been a professor, teacher, scientist, musician, artist—anything that could possibly indicate that a collection of books or periodicals might be up for grabs—he wrote to the family about it. Usually a collector's family, if they don't want the books themselves, puts the library up for auction or sells it to a dealer, since these sources are the most accessible and will take the entire collection en bloc. But if you make yourself known to them, the family may consider selling the collection to you.

If you do write to the family, remember that they are in mourning. Your letter should be polite, low-keyed, and respectful. Discreetly inquire if there is a library, and if it is for sale. If so, you would be interested in seeing the books with the hope of purchasing them, and would they inform you at their convenience if you could view the books? Always end the letter with a sincere condolence.

If you get to see the books and you find that the collection is of interest to you, buy it outright if you are in a position to do so. Even if some of the books aren't quite in your area of collecting, you should still consider buying the entire collection, because you can always trade, sell, or auction the books that are not of immediate interest. Remember, the larger the collection, the less it will cost you per volume. You can recoup the difference when the parts are sold or traded.

If the collection is too large for your budget or space, then select the volumes that interest you and make an offer for those only; you must expect to pay more per volume for your selectivity. If you are just starting out and not experienced enough to make an outright offer, then be honest and inform the person that you have noted the titles of interest. Ask if those books can be put aside for a few days. You then have the time to research them, as you would if you were readying yourself for an upcoming auction, and to come back with a figure that is accurate and fair.

Don't try to bargain for too low a price, because most likely you won't be the only person looking at the books. Probably the estate will have contacted a few dealers as well, so the prices will be competitive. Remember, you are in a better position than the trade; you can offer more because you aren't buying for resale. So be fair; I have found in twenty years of buying that the fairer you are, the better your chances of getting what you want.

DID YOU KNOW THAT YOUR PUBLIC LIBRARY MAY SELL BOOKS?

Actually, public, private, college, university, and professional libraries all sell books on occasion. Libraries are given books as donations, or are willed them by friends and patrons. Some of these books may not fit in with the collections, or they may be duplicates of books the library already has. Libraries also acquire duplicates through faulty cataloguing and purchasing. Once or twice a year they may have a sale in order to get rid of these items.

Some of the larger colleges and universities, such as Brandeis and Vassar, have very extensive book sales. Such sales are advertised in the local papers, or in trade journals such as the *AB Bookman's Weekly*; or if you are a friend (donor) of the library, you will most likely be informed in one of the library publications. Other libraries sell their duplicates more discreetly through auctions and by circulating lists of duplicates to booksellers. If you are a patron, user, or otherwise in touch with a library that has special collections in your area of collecting interest, contact the librarian and tell him or her that you are interested in buying items in your field; or at least try to get on the mailing list the library uses to announce sales. Librarians may offer you their better duplicates if you are known to them. They want to keep their friends on the best of terms, hoping that in the future these patrons will leave their collections to the library.

Public or private, a library sale is an excellent opportunity for finding books of interest. Try to arrive as early as possible on the opening day so that you can view the books at the same time as the dealers. Remember that most library books are marked by the library on the spine, title page, half-title page—and sometimes throughout. If the volume is illustrated, there may be a stamp on the margins of the plates, or perhaps a perforated stamp on every other leaf. Check the volume through carefully, and if the markings or condition disturb you, don't buy it.

INTERNATIONAL BOOK FAIRS

International book fairs are excellent ways of meeting dealers, seeing their stock, talking to them in person, getting on their mailing lists, socializing, and last but not least, *buying*.

In the past few years, book fairs have grown in size and importance. The Antiquarian Booksellers Association of America used to sponsor a book fair in New York City in odd years and in California—San Francisco and Los Angeles alternated as the sites—in even years. In England, there was one major annual fair, the London Antiquarian Book Fair, sponsored by the Antiquarian Booksellers Association (British), and less extensive local fairs.

All of these fairs were small. The fair I organized for the ABAA's Middle Atlantic Chapter in New York in 1966 had only twenty-four exhibitors. But in 1978 there were two book fairs in New York City alone, both in April, the first at the Americana Hotel, with some 120 dealers exhibiting, the second at the Plaza Hotel, with some seventy dealers exhibiting. (I exhibited in both; it was a very hectic month.) The same year, in September, there was an international book fair in Zurich, which I attended, an ABAA-sponsored book fair in Boston, where I exhibited, fairs in Chicago and Los Angeles, and one in Toronto sponsored by the Antiquarian Booksellers' Association of Canada. Most of these fairs are now annual events.

Dealers from all over the world attend international book fairs, so the fairs give you a great chance to meet foreign booksellers. If you know librarians or collectors who will be attending, you can arrange to meet them there, too. Book fairs are both exciting and informative. You will see books, prints, autographs, and ephemera on display there that you never had the opportunity to see before, or perhaps that you didn't even know existed.

To get the most out of a fair, make some advance plans. Trade journals like the *AB Bookman's Weekly* usually publish a list of the dealers who are going to exhibit at the fair. If time permits, write to those dealers who you know will have items in your areas of interest and inform them that you will be attending the fair on the opening night; if they have anything of interest to you, would they put it aside until you see the titles (some dealers will comply with such a request and others won't), or could you have their catalogue or list before the fair opens? Many dealers publish a listing of the items they will exhibit, but don't be surprised if you don't receive the listing before the opening, because many dealers don't like to distribute their fair lists in advance. If you are lucky and do receive an advance copy, go over the listings carefully. Check those items you are really interested in and their prices. Go to the fair on opening night, examine the books you have checked off, and if they're what you want, buy them there and then. If you don't, they might be sold before you get back to the booth. Good items can go very fast at a fair.

The *AB* also publishes groundplans of the rooms where a major fair is to be held. On the groundplan, the booths of the various dealers are marked and numbered. Before the fair opens, survey the layout and mark the dealers in your area of interest. On opening night, visit their booths in the order of their likely importance for you. Leave the others for the next day; book fairs usually last three or four days, and there is usually a lull the day after opening night. Take good advantage of this lull to talk to the dealers in your collecting area. Tell them about your collection. Ask them to keep you informed of items of interest. Take their lists or catalogues, leave your card, and ask to be put on their mailing lists. Give one dealer a listing of your desiderata; remember, the rule for search services is one dealer at a time for a fixed time.

If you have books to sell, you can give the dealers a list of the items. Don't bring the books themselves with you; you won't be allowed to bring them into the fair, and it's *schleppy* to try and sell them outside the door.

OTHER SHOWS AND MARKETS

Universities, colleges, schools, churches, and synagogues may sponsor book fairs as part of their fund-raising activities. These are smaller in scale than international book fairs; perhaps twenty or thirty dealers, who represent the local book trade, will exhibit.

These fairs are announced in local newspapers, trade journals, and direct mailings, and they offer excellent opportunities to see and buy less expensive but just as important items. Last year at the May Fair sponsored by Grace Church School in Greenwich Village, where my two daughters, Liz and Michèle, went to school, I bought a $15 book for 50¢.

Then there are the shows primarily of other objects which also have a few books for sale. Antique shows, for example, usually have a few exhibitors who specialize in books relating to the decorative arts; or dealers exhibiting other wares have books on the items exhibited—dealers in china usually have some books on china, and so on. Most cities that have conventions, shows, and conferences publish an annual or seasonal listing of the events that will take place, and you can select the ones that may show books in your area of interest. Write to the local chamber of commerce, convention bureau, or hotel association and ask to be put on the mailing list so that you can find out when the event is scheduled and plan ahead.

THE NEWSPAPERS

Newspapers have several sections that can be useful to you. First, every good daily newspaper should contain a book review column, and some have several pages devoted to books. *The New York Times* has a complete Book Review section on Sundays, which you can subscribe to separately from the rest of the paper. Then there are the special journals about books, such as the *New York Review of Books*.

Read the reviews of new books and the articles on books and authors if they concern your interests in the slightest degree. Order the new books you want, and note the prices of all books in your area of interest; when the title is out of print, you will have the record on the verso of your index card.

Then read the advertisements. Among the books for sale will be remainders, slow-selling books that the publishers have sold to distributors, who in turn have sold them to discount bookstores such as Marboro or Barnes & Noble, which sell them at retail at half the original price or less. A remaindered book may be a good book for your reference or your collection, and it is in new to mint condition. These books are no longer available from the publisher, so technically they are out of print; once the distributors' and booksellers' stock is exhausted, which it normally is within a few weeks or months, the remainders are also factually out of print. Several years ago, I bought eight copies of Man Ray's autobiography, *Self Portrait*, from a remainder house (available to the trade only); Marboro had it at the same price—$1. I recently sold my last copy for $35.

The book section also carries ads for booksellers, and you may find a dealer in your area whom you hadn't known about previously. There are also catalogue offers that you might be interested in.

Also read your newspaper's section on business opportunities. Occasionally a bookstore is up for sale, and there is a slight possibility that if the owner hasn't sold the stock, he or she may be willing to sell a section of it to you if you offer more than a dealer would; or if the stock has been sold, you can try to get the name of the dealer and inquire if the books you are interested in are for sale en bloc.

You can also use the newspapers to advertise for the books you need. With a little practice, you can compose your own small advertisement. One way to begin is to read all the classified ads in the various papers and journals and see what makes them effective. See which ones are repeated in issue after issue; these are the ones that have been successful. Model your ad on them. You can say, for example,

Urgently needed: 1st ed. of J. Thomas, *Night Ends*

or

Urgently wanted: all 1st eds. of J. Thomas with d.j.

or

Everything on cookie cutters in good cond. needed, except . . .

If you do not want to give your name, use a box number and the journal will forward replies to you.

BOOKSELLERS' JOURNALS

The major booksellers' trade journals, such as the *AB*, won't accept ads for books wanted from private collectors, but you can find information about books for sale there. Read the "books for sale" section as soon as you get your copy and telephone your order immediately, following up with a confirmation by letter. Forget about ordering books advertised in foreign trade journals unless you receive them by airmail—otherwise, the books will most likely be sold by the time you read the ad.

If there are books advertised that you already have in your collection, note the price, the date, and the dealer for your future reference on the back of the 3 × 5 card you have catalogued the title on. If you haven't catalogued the item yet, put a slip of paper into the book with this information, and be sure to copy it onto the verso of the card when you catalogue the book. If the book is advertised in a foreign journal, translate the currency into dollars when listing the price; it's also a good idea to list the approximate cost of the postage, handling, and bank transfer charges. (An average cost is $6 for an octavo volume sent by ordinary surface mail, registered.)

SPECIALIZED JOURNALS

In specialized journals, there are usually ads offering books for sale in the area the journal covers. For example, I advertise in *Art News*. Most specialized journals also have a section that reviews new books relating to the subjects covered by the magazine. Read these reviews and decide whether you need these titles for your collection, for your reference, or simply for your general knowledge.

TRADE AND PROFESSIONAL JOURNALS AND ORGANIZATIONS

Trade and professional journals are published for people in a particular line of work. You are probably already aware of the trade journals in your field; you may even subscribe to one or more. If you are collecting books about your profession, you have half the problem solved. You can read reviews of new books in your trade journal, and advertise in it for out-of-print books that you want.

If your work is your collecting interest, write to your professional organization and inquire about journals in the field; there may be some you don't know about. Then write to the publishers of these periodicals and ask for a sample copy.

Some professional organizations have book clubs, through some of which members can purchase books at a discount. If there isn't a book club, you might start one. Attend the next meeting and see if there are other collectors there who might be interested. Take up the subject at the meeting, when the speaker asks if there is any new business to be discussed. It is amazing what you can do to further your ambitions in the collecting area by just making yourself available to opportunities.

THRIFT SHOPS AND OTHER BARGAIN POSSIBILITIES

Once you realize that you want to buy materials for your collection and you keep this in mind in all your travels, excursions, vacations, and spare-time activities, you will find yourself spending many happy hours exploring for books in the most unlikely places. Often you will find something wonderful for your collection. Occasionally you may find a bargain. One of Italy's leading booksellers got started in the book trade when, as a junk paper dealer, he discovered a group of George Washington's letters in a heap of refuse and sold them to the Library of Congress. A British dealer I know discovered a group of Robert Burns's letters in a pile of papers he bought from a used paper dealer. So these things do happen, and you may be lucky.

Many collectors haunt the thrift shops sponsored by colleges, hospitals, and other institutions. Thrift shops sometimes are given books, and they may sell them for bargain prices.

Then there are flea markets. It may take awhile to discover who has what, but you will find that many exhibitors also sell books. Farmers' markets now attract many antique dealers, and these people, too, may have books of interest for your collection either on display or in their shops. Leave your card and ask them to inform you if anything new arrives or if they see interesting books in their wanderings. You might offer them a finder's fee of 5 to 10 percent if they come upon a good collection that they don't want to purchase outright. (In other words, if you pay $40 for the books, they get $4 for having located the books and informed you of their whereabouts.)

In New York and other cities, there are street fairs sponsored by local neighborhoods. Visit these fairs. They are lots of fun, and you never know what goodies will be unearthed.

Garage sales are also places to look for books—and their accessories, such as bookcases, book stands, and bookends. Once while visiting a friend in Connecticut, I stopped at a garage sale and bought a real oak bookcase with glass doors for a nominal price.

Caveat: At thrift shops, flea markets, street fairs, etc., prices are not always low. Sometimes you can wind up paying more than you would if you bought the item elsewhere. But if you are knowledgeable about the books you want, you won't be cheated—and you may even find a bargain.

CHAPTER 8

Caring for Your Books

If you are going to spend the time, money, and effort to build a fine collection, then spend the time, money, and effort to care for your books so that they are kept in as good a condition as possible. Remember, their value depends to a great degree on their physical condition.

If you are just starting to collect, you are in a good position to set up a system of storing and caring for the books that will be easy for you to manage as well as safe for the books. If you already have a collection, it still isn't too late to bring a little more order, caution, and care into your collecting activities. The first thing to do is to get the books out of the cartons, valises, suitcases, and trunks and onto the shelf. It's bad for their health for books to lie around in a haphazard fashion.

In many respects, books should be cared for like good vintage wine. They should be kept in a relatively cool, dry, and dark environment, and undisturbed until called for.

KEEP COOL, DIM, AND DRY

By cool, I mean a constant temperature of 68° Fahrenheit or less—pretty hard for the average collector to maintain, but a guideline for you in placing the books in a spot that comes as close to this figure as possible. What this means in common sense terms is simply this: Do not place your shelves in an area that is heat-producing—*never* near a fireplace, a stove, an oven, a boiler, a radiator, or a wall that carries hot water pipes. Walls with pipes that carry water or steam can "sweat," creating moisture on the surface of the wall which can damage your books; even worse for your books, these walls may develop leaks.

Keep your books away from direct exposure to windows, and away from strong artificial light. Too much light can turn pages yellow and cause bindings to fade. Keep this in mind and don't place lamps next to your bookshelves, or—even worse—attach spotlights to bookcases. The less direct light, the better. Darkness is good for books.

By dry, I mean the humidity in the air; and if you live in New York, you know how humid it can get. The ideal relative humidity would be around 50 percent. Paper absorbs moisture. A very moist atmosphere can wrinkle pages, warp covers, and, in extreme cases, even cause mildew. On the other hand, too little moisture in the air can make the pages brittle. That's another reason for keeping your books away from the radiator; steam heat has a drying as well as a heating effect.

I don't want to be an alarmist, but if what I have just said sends you rushing to the attic or the basement to rescue your books, all the better. With a little forethought and planning, you can arrange for the books to be shelved in areas that have a minimum exposure to heat, light, and moisture, and a minimum possibility of drastic changes in these elements.

SAFETY FIRST

Books as a rule do not burn, because they are usually compressed with other books and there isn't sufficient oxygen to feed a fire. But they are damaged by smoke, water, heat, and sometimes by firemen. It's a good idea to buy a fire extinguisher for your library. Get one that uses chemicals or foam. Never use water to extinguish a fire in your library.

BOOKCASES AND SHELVES

The best holder for books is a bookcase with doors or sliding panels, preferably glass-fronted. This receptacle provides protection on all sides and therefore reduces the amount of light, heat, moisture, and dust that reaches the books. It also reduces unnecessary handling and interference by guests, children, pets, insects, and other intruders.

Dust is a big problem, especially in cities. If you wish to use open bookcases or shelves, I have found a relatively inexpensive solution. Buy roll-up, slotted blinds of bamboo or wood that have cords to raise and lower them. These blinds are available in many sizes, or they can be cut down to size. Fasten the blind to the top of the bookcase so that it can be rolled down and act as a natural barrier to dust, light, and prying hands. When you wish to display the books, you can easily roll up the blinds. But please make sure that no books are protruding beyond the edge of the shelf—otherwise you will damage the extended surfaces when you raise or lower the blinds. You can mount the blinds away from the bookcase by using curtain-rod holders or hooks that screw into the top of the bookcase. This will provide a few extra inches between the books and the blinds.

The size of your shelves is important. Except for folios and large quartos, the majority of your books can be shelved on shelves one foot deep and one foot high. If you have oversize books or portfolios, then be sure to provide some wider shelves so that the books can rest horizontally on a surface as large as or larger than their width. Never let an oversized volume rest on a surface that is narrower than the volume itself. And don't pile too many oversized volumes on top of one another. Their combined weight can damage the bindings of the bottom volumes. The best solution is to have the large shelf you use for the oversized volumes divided into smaller horizontal units, each containing one or at the most two volumes per unit, with enough space for the books to be removed and inserted easily.

Remember that books are heavy and that when they are placed

side by side they exert pressure on the shelf in two directions, both down and out (away from the wall). For these reasons, it is important to secure your shelves solidly. If you plan to attach bookshelves to a wall, make sure that the wall is strong enough to support the weight. Locate the beams. With a ¼-inch or ⅛-inch electric drill, drill into the beam; plaster alone isn't strong enough to support the weight. Wood beams are easy to drill through, and you can buy bits for your drill that will drill through steel and concrete beams as well; make sure you buy the correct bit for the material you are drilling.

Use brackets to support your shelves. Make sure the shelves are supported every three or four feet so that the weight of the books doesn't cause them to warp; warped shelves disturb the upright position of the books and make them tip, causing stress on the bindings. Use screws and anchors to attach the brackets to the wall. The anchors must be the right size for the screws. All these materials are available at your local hardware store, lumberyard, building supply store, or home center. Ask the clerk to give you the correct bit, anchors, and matching screws.

If you are constructing your own shelves and are using untreated lumber, sand the shelves on both top and bottom as well as on the sides. Do it well, so that no rough spots, edges, or splinters remain to damage the books' bindings or edges. Use a sealer after sanding the wood, and check to see that your surface is very smooth. It may take two or three coats of sealer, varnish, or paint to finish the surface smoothly.

Never use enamel paint on bookshelves. Enamel dries very slowly and is very susceptible to climatic changes. I once painted a bookcase with blue enamel and waited what I thought was a very long time—three weeks, to be exact—before placing oversized bound volumes horizontally in it. After a week or so, I tried to remove the bottom volume and found that it had grown attached to the surface. I removed the top volumes, waited another week, and tried again. It still resisted me, but I finally pried it loose—and with it, some of the blue enamel.

Provide a base for your bookcase, or, with bookshelves, make sure the bottom shelf is off the floor. More bottoms of bindings inadvertently get waxed, shellacked, washed, or splashed than you can possibly imagine. A safe distance is six inches to a foot from the floor.

SHELVING BOOKS, PERIODICALS, AND EPHEMERA

It is extremely important to have your volumes upright at all times to reduce the wear on the bindings and inner hinges. Books have a tendency to sway or tilt when you remove a volume. If the book is absent for a long time, the space will slowly disappear as the books on either side turn to fill it. For this reason, always replace the volume as soon as possible, or fill the space with another volume. You may use bookends, but paste felt or another soft material on the side that goes against the book. Don't use those metal bookends that have a bottom extending under the volume; usually these bottoms jab into the book.

Folios should be on their sides, lying flat on a surface big enough for the volume. Make sure you have a surface under all your books; don't let them hang over the shelf either horizontally or vertically. The parts that are unsupported will expand while the parts that are supported by the shelf and the weight of other volumes won't, causing warping or damage to the binding. If you must pile folios on top of one another, overlap the spines so that the spine of the bottom volume is covered with the fore-edge (the side opposite the spine) of the next volume; limit the pile to two or at the very most three volumes, so that the bindings don't scratch one another. (If you have a shelf high enough to accomodate folios, then you can stand them up; but make sure that they are the same or nearly the same size, are standing firmly, and are supported by other volumes on either side, or by bookends that can provide support without scratching or damaging the last volume.)

In most cases, books can be shelved in their bindings or dust jackets without any additional protective cover. There are acid-free papers that you can use to make your own covers for books that are handled more frequently than usual. Such papers are manufactured by the Hollinger Corporation and can be ordered through Talas, a division of Technical Library Service, 130 Fifth Avenue, New York, NY 10011. Avoid the slipcase, the box that is enclosed on all sides except the spine and that you have to push the book into. This type of case creates a partial vacuum when you push the volume into place so that it's hard to remove the book, causing unnecessary wear on the upper and lower parts of the spine. I have seen volumes literally stuck within their slipcase. One way to remove a book in a case like this is to puncture the closed spine of the slipcase with a needle so as to create an air hole that will relieve the pressure on the volume; but be very careful with the needle if you have a book inside the slipcase, or you might damage the book's fore-edge. If you do have slipcases, remove the volumes from them right now, and make the air holes.

The best type of box for books is the so-called clam shell box, which has an attached cover. These boxes are built to size; take a look at one at your local library, and then try constructing your own.

Periodicals, if unbound, should be stored horizontally on their sides. If you have a single issue of a periodical, it is best to protect it in a folder, such as a manila file folder. If you own a run of unbound numbers, say ten to twelve issues, then you can buy magazine files. These are special open-backed files designed to hold periodicals upright. They come in different sizes, from 8½ × 4 × 6 to 12¾ × 4 × 10⅜, and can be ordered from your stationery store. If you want to spend a little more, you can buy a deluxe magazine file that is entirely enclosed. If you are going to refer to the periodicals constantly, the closed file is better, since the likelihood of spines and edges rubbing one another when removed and replaced is kept to a minimum.

Do not place heavy runs of a periodical on an upper shelf. Stack them as low as possible in your bookcase, where the weight will not exert the pull out and down it would on a higher shelf. Or else distribute the run over a few shelves.

You will also want to keep all the ephemera associated with your books. If a dust wrapper, or dust jacket, was issued and you have it—keep it. A publisher's prospectus; a price list; a letter from the author; an invitation to a publishing party, an opening, a cocktail party; the author's signature; the author's comments; the publisher's release—whatever is associated with the book adds to the story of the book and is valuable for its place in the unfolding of the literary history of the author, publisher, and contemporary milieu. These so-called accessories provide you and the literary world with additional insight into the events surrounding the existence of the work, its place in the history of the author's development, and the evolution of the literary history concerned with the title.

Preserve these items with all the care of an archaeologist who uncovers a hidden treasure. A dust jacket should be stored in its natural place—on the book. A single sheet of paper having to do with the book—a letter, for example—can be kept in the book. But nothing bulky must be put in the book, because that would harm the binding. Keep other ephemera, unfolded, in a paper envelope next to the book. Don't use plastic or cellophane envelopes—the papers can't breathe through them.

HANDLE WITH CARE

The first rule to remember when you are unpacking, cataloguing, or reading your books is that your hands must be clean and dry, or even better still, clad in white cotton gloves that can be bought very inexpensively in hardware stores. Dirty fingers can leave their impressions on light-colored bindings, jackets, wrappers, and papers. Oil from your hands or face (unconsciously, you may wipe it with your hands because of the dust generated from the unpacking or shelving) can be transferred to the books. Never smoke while handling books; ashes have a way of diving onto the books, there to be smudged into the paper. Never eat or drink while handling books, or have food or liquids near the area you are working in—not on the table, chair, cartons, or shelves. It's very frustrating to have a rare book splattered with coffee or a dropped book landing in a bowl of soup and splattering the soup over other books in the vicinity. You know, there are days when you seem to be accident prone. Don't go near your books on those days. Leave the unpacking, cataloguing, and viewing to days when you feel in top-notch shape, clear, relaxed, aware, and unhurried. This is the optimum condition in which to approach your collection. You and your books will be the better for it.

When you read your books, be careful about how you mark your place. The best bookmark is a very fine, thin, white ribbon. Other bookmarks tend to break or scratch the pages. And please— no paperclips; they mark and tear the page and are hazardous to the binding.

Bookplates (also called *"ex libris"*) are other objects that can be nice to look at in themselves but are damaging to books. If the bookplate identifies the book as part of a famous collection, it may enhance the book's value; otherwise, it reduces it. If you try to remove a bookplate, part of the page it's on usually comes with it. If for some reason you absolutely must use a bookplate, use one with an adhesive backing that is easy to remove.

Now, provide a space where you can read or look at your books in comfort and safety. Get a desk or table or fold-out shelf large enough to support your largest volume, opened. This surface should be close enough to your bookshelves to minimize the possibility of an accident on the way. Dropped books can be severely damaged.

Your desk or table can also be used for cataloguing and un-

packing. It is a great asset for a library, and it will come in handy
on many occasions.

HOW TO CLEAN AND PRESERVE YOUR BOOKS

When you unpack your books, dust them if necessary, but do
it as gently as possible. Hold the book by its fore-edge and dust
with a very soft cloth. *Never* shake the books. Once the books
are on the shelves, an occasional gentle dusting is again all that
is usually necessary. Do it by hand; don't succumb to the temp-
tation to use a vacuum cleaner.

Leather bindings should be oiled periodically to prevent crack-
ing (except for pigskin and vellum; oiling may change their color).
Use a soft cloth and a commercially prepared dressing such as the
one sold by Talas (their address is 130 Fifth Avenue, New York,
NY 10011) or the British Museum Leather Dressing manufactured
by the Amend Drug & Chemical Company, 83 Cordier Street,
Irvington, NJ 07111. These dressings are quite expensive, but you
need only a small amount at a time.

REPAIRS

At one time collectors would have all their books rebound to
suit their own tastes; nowadays, many people believe that the
natural state of a book is the most desirable one—the way the
book was originally published or issued, whether bound or in
wrappers, in sheets, in installments, or whatever, is how these
collectors and libraries want it.

But even purists must occasionally send books to the binder's
for repairs. If the job is a small one—say, the binding must be
tightened, or a cloth binding repaired—or the books are inexpensive ones, perhaps for your reference library, a local binder
can do it. For more expensive books, the repairs should be done
by an expert. Contact your local museum, college, or university
library and ask them to recommend one. If the expert lives out

of town, write to him or her, explain the problem, and ask the fees. After you hear from the expert, you can send him or her the book by mail.

If you agree that the original state is the most desirable, then ask the expert to keep as much of the original binding intact as is possible.

ANOTHER WORD ABOUT CATALOGUING

In Chapter 3 I outlined a procedure for cataloguing which I recommended as a guide to keeping up with your new acquisitions as well as for organizing the books you already had. You should be well into this system by now. If not, go back and reread that chapter. Remember, a short pencil is better than a long memory. Another important thing to remember is that consistency in cataloguing is essential. For these reasons the cataloguing system you select should be one you can grow with; the one I have outlined in Chapter 3 is flexible enough to withstand the maximum growth.

Your catalogue cards are very important for your collection as well as for such things as tax records, insurance, and appraisals. Keep your catalogue cards in a safe place, and don't let them leave your premises. Mine never do. They did once, when I began. I had one set of cards and gave them to the printer who was setting up my catalogue. After he finished, he mailed them back, but they never reached me—they were lost in the mail. Although they were insured for a nominal amount, I still was left to figure out what stock I had by using the printed catalogue and my shelving system. Luckily it was just my second year in business, and my stock was relatively small; if it happened today, I would cut my wrists.

But it wouldn't happen today. I never allow my original stock cards to leave the premises, and you shouldn't, either. In fact, if you want to really play it safe, it is an excellent idea to have your cards duplicated and keep one set in your deposit box, or another safe place away from where you keep your originals, in case of fire or theft.

Shelving is also an important part of cataloguing. Remember to mark your shelves as you catalogue your collection. This is especially true if others are going to handle the books (something I don't recommend). My stock is arranged with a number and a letter for each shelf. Since my business is mail order, I do not get many browsers, and I ask those who do come up to leave the books aside, so my assistants and I can reshelve them ourselves later. So the problem of taking out a volume and returning it to the wrong shelf is minimal; still, some books are always misplaced.

Another suggestion that can help when you receive new books that are awaiting cataloguing is to have a shelf or two just for uncatalogued books. We have two aisles, containing ninety-one shelves in all, just for books that have to be catalogued. We have alphabetized these shelves so that we can put the new acquisitions on them by author or artist—or title, if a periodical. Let's be practical. If you don't have the time to catalogue what you receive right away, at least you can see what you have purchased and keep those books in good condition by getting them unpacked, off the floor, and upright on a shelf until you can catalogue them and put them in their proper place on the right shelf in the collection. Make sure you put a slip of paper with the date you bought the book, the dealer's name, and the price into each uncatalogued book.

I deliberately didn't mention in Chapter 3 that you can also buy commercially printed cards for your titles from the Library of Congress. I don't recommend this because it's important for you to do the cataloguing yourself, at least in the beginning. Cataloguing will teach you how to read dealers' catalogues, remainder house lists, and publishers' announcements. It will also help you become familiar with your books. Before you even read the book, you will find information and discover references and passages that interest you. This familiarity is indispensable when you are browsing in bookstores, reading catalogues and announcements away from home, or discussing your collection with others at meetings and fairs. You will begin to develop the catalogue mind. You will visualize the item and its characteristics.

I have never wanted to expand my business to the point of forfeiting the pleasure of handling the books myself. Even if I do not catalogue each book I purchase now, I make sure that my assistant leaves the card in the book so that I can compare the two—not just to check the accuracy of the description, but so that I have the opportunity of familiarizing myself with the item. Once I have handled it, I remember it. Once you have catalogued it, you will, too.

My old boss, Paul Gottschalk, whenever he went to a party and got a little high, would corner some librarian and recite all the publications of the Akademie der Wissenschaften, Berlin, to the utter amazement of the poor captive—it would take a couple of hours, if he weren't dragged away before he could finish. But his familiarity with the publications was impressive. A book that you catalogue is a book that you know. Why give up this pleasure?

FILING

It is important to keep all the papers, catalogues, lists, and letters that you have concerning books on order. It is also important to be able to find them when the books are received so that you can compare the books with the invoice, catalogue, or letter offer or description. For these reasons a filing system is important. If you do not have room for a three-drawer metal office cabinet or don't want one in your home, think about getting a wooden or plastic one, whichever blends into your decor; the top can be used as a table.

Label the top drawer "Ordered Items—On the Way." Buy manila file folders, and label each one with a letter of the alphabet. Place all the material relating to your order—the catalogue, list, or letter, or its important part, together with a carbon of your reply—in the appropriate file. If the seller's name is a commercial one like Biblios, file it in the "B" file. If the company is called by the bookseller's name, file under the last name. Many European booksellers have "Libreria" or "Librairie" or "Antiquariat" in front of the name—don't file those under "L" or "A," but under the actual name of the dealer.

When the books arrive, remove the materials from the file and copy them onto a catalogue card; or at least retain the description and place it inside the book or, if it's bulky, next to the book on the uncatalogued shelf. You can also cut out the entry, or photocopy it if you do not want to destroy the catalogue, and paste or glue it to the back of the catalogue card. Indicate the cost on the card in pencil until all the costs are in—the exchange rate, conversion charges, postage, telephone, etc.

If the catalogue is important to you, keep it; important catalogues are valuable reference tools. Keep your catalogues together in a magazine file. Organize them by dealer or by subject—say, photography, architecture, sports, birds, etc.

You can use the second drawer of the file cabinet for paid bills. Keep all your invoices for at least four years, and preferably longer. They will be invaluable for proving your costs when selling, auctioning, or evaluating your collection. The label for this drawer should read, "Paid Bills from ———— to ————." Use the same alphabetical setup and the same type of manila folders.

If you have additional drawers, they may be used for subscriptions, supplies, and/or materials.

INSURANCE

Perhaps you don't think your collection looks like much yet. You may have just located the books, or just been given them, or just woken up to the fact that you own them; but the sooner you realize that they are worth something, the sooner you will insure them, since they are now an investment.

If the collection is worth more than $250, you should insure the books. The reason I say $250 is that most policies have a deductible of from $250-$500; that is, you are not covered for the first $250 to $500. This makes the policy cheaper.

Insurance is very expensive today. There are basically two types of insurance policies. One insures at the fair market price, the other at cost-plus—this means simply what you have paid for the book plus, say, 20 percent. Insurance companies don't want you to make a profit on them, so they are very conservative; as they should be, since the more they have to pay out, the more the premiums go up. I have cost-plus insurance, which has lower premiums, but if you are in a position to cover your books at the fair market price, I would recommend that you do so.

Fair market insurance carries an added responsibility for you in that you will have to keep very close track of the prices of your books and re-evaluate them each year before your premium comes due. You will also have to have proof of an evaluation or appraisal (see pp. 126–128); for that matter, if you sell a part of your collection, you will have to report the sale, the amount received, and the books sold, so that the insurance company will have proof of the fair market value of the diminished collection. This is one reason for noting all current prices on the verso of the catalogue card or on a separate card attached to the catalogue card.

But at least with this type of insurance, if your books are lost, stolen, or damaged in a flood or fire, you receive the fair market value of the book. With cost-plus insurance, you will receive only what you paid for the item plus whatever percentage the insurance company has agreed to of the cost price. If you bought the book for $50, you would receive perhaps $60 ($50 + 20% = $60). This means that if you purchased the book within the last year or even two, you might just come out even if you want to replace the copy; but if you bought the book five, seven, or ten years ago, because of inflation you will be losing approximately 50 percent on the five-year-old purchase, 70 percent on the seven-year, and 90 percent on the ten-year-old purchase should you wish to replace the item at the current market price.

You will be shocked to find that a book you bought three or four years ago may now be going for double the price, but this seems to be the way inflation has hit us. You will also appreciate the problems dealers have with replacing their good stock. For these reasons, I would make sure that the insurance value of your collection is as close to the current fair market price as possible. You will have to decide what is easier for your pocketbook.

Talk to your insurance agent. If you own your own home, it is possible to include a clause in your home policy to include your collection. If you are an apartment dweller, it may be cheaper to include your collection in your coverage for household effects.

But do insure the collection as soon as possible. Always include those books that you have purchased and that are on the way to you, because they will be arriving within a relatively short time; if they fall into the insured year, you should notify your broker and buy additional coverage if necessary. The books may be insured in transit, but once they arrive, they're your responsibility. I know one collector who bought $4,200 in auction from England and failed to notify his broker because he thought it could wait until the books were catalogued. As things turned out, he was out of town when the books arrived, there was a fire in the house, and the books literally went up in smoke.

It might be a good idea for your broker to visit your house or apartment before you take out the policy. As well as explaining the policy, the broker can, if you request it, recommend areas in your home that are the least hazardous for storing books.

IN SUM

Once you have set up the systems I have outlined here, you will have no problems in maintaining the normal cycle of ordering, cataloguing, storing, and caring for your books. Necessary jobs will be done expediently, and you will have more time to enjoy the collection itself.

CHAPTER 9

Shaping Your Collection

You are now on your way to filling in the collection. Let the collection develop gradually. You will find that it is never complete—that you are always searching for some elusive volume. I remember what Walter Grossmann told me when he was still librarian at Harvard. He said that although the Harvard libraries may have 90 percent of what they need, they search for the remaining 10 percent with 90 percent of their effort. When the pursuit is in your own behalf, your effort will be greater still. But then, it's the pursuit itself that's so exciting.

Here are some guides to help you in the chase.

LEARNING FROM OTHERS

At the beginning of their careers, artists are often attracted to certain masters of their metier. They may not know why consciously; but really it is because the master's vision agrees with their own. The student is drawn to one who has succeeded in expressing the vision that is dormant, but nonetheless present, in him or herself.

In the presence of a great collection, the beginning collector—

and even the more experienced one—can find the same inspiration that the beginning artist feels in the presence of a masterpiece of his or her art. I remember the first time I saw Hans Bolliger's collection. I was in Bern to attend a book auction at Kornfeld & Klipstein's auction house. Hans Bolliger had catalogued the books for sale and was acting as auctioneer in the afternoon session.

Mr. Bolliger is an eminent art historian, bibliographer, bookseller, and friend of many of the surrealists and dadaists. When I was an undergraduate student of art history, I used to think how great it would be to study with either of two men: one was Bernard Karpel, then the librarian of the Museum of Modern Art, whom I later got to know, and who was very helpful and sympathetic during my starting years as a bookseller; and the other was Hans Bolliger. I finally met Mr. Bolliger in Bern at the pre-auction inspection of the books. I was very pleased to learn that he knew of me through my catalogues. He invited me to his flat to see his collection.

My experience that evening was one I shall never forget. It was a collector's dream. The books were just the ones I would collect. Mr. Bolliger's tastes and mine are similar; he loves and collects the artists, writers, and art of the twentieth century. There they were, all in fine to excellent condition, most in their original bindings, all inscribed to Hans Bolliger—either with drawings on the front flyleaves or long dedications. Where there were limited editions, he had the lowest numbers—many were the artists' copies, or the prepublication or subscribers' editions. Some of the books I had never seen in person, only in bibliographic citations; others were completely unknown to me. I inspected all the books with care and awe, pausing only to remark occasionally how beautiful a work was, or how nice it was of Max Ernst or Max Bill to have written so feeling a dedication.

It was an experience that comes rarely in one's life, to see a great collection of twentieth-century art and illustrated books assembled by one of the most knowledgeable historians of the movements, books that were beautiful in themselves, significant to the artists' development, and milestones in the art of the book. By the time I said good night to Mr. Bolliger and his charming wife, around midnight, I was heady with excitement and truly inspired. I vowed that from then on my books, too, would be the choicest items, meaningful in terms of the artist and the art of the book.

Any collection you see can help you, whether it is within your area of interest or not, whether it excites you or not. Every collection has a personality that is unique. If you can perceive this uniqueness, this special character, then you will discern its strength and its scope and know whether it's important to you.

But a collection that excites you can place you firmly on the road to self-discovery. Explore the reasons for your enchantment. Ask yourself why it is so exciting. If you can analyze the elements that turned you on, then, my dear collector, you are on your way to knowing what books or areas have personal meaning for you. You will know what you want to collect as well as what you don't want to collect. Now you have the bull by the horns; and as frightening as this may be, by golly it's exciting!

BACK TO THE LIBRARY

A great place to see book collections is the library. To find out which college, university, museum, public, and/or special libraries have collections in your field of interest, consult *Subject Collections*, a book by Lee Ash and Denis Lorenz published by the R.R. Bowker Company; it is most likely available at your local library.

If the library you are interested in is in your city, telephone; if it's out of town, write and tell them when you will be there. Arrange an appointment with the librarian or keeper of the collection you are interested in. It's also a good idea to specify particular books you are interested in seeing so that they will be set aside for you.

So much is out there for you to avail yourself of, if you only take the first step. Once you have broken the ice, it will be easy. Make the commitment, and allow the experiences to unfold.

In all my years with books, I have never been rejected by a library. I have visited dozens of college, museum, university, and public libraries. By and large, all the librarians I have met have been courteous and attentive. Why? Because I prepared the framework prior to my visit. I knew what type of collection they had. I made an appointment in advance. When I got there, I looked at the books and inquired about the collections, their funding, and the plans for future collection development. I came to see, to learn, and, finally, to sell. I wasn't always successful in the latter objective. But I learned a lot about libraries and the way they are administered, which came in handy when I sold to or bought from other libraries or even other booksellers or collectors. If you are open and receptive, you will learn a lot, too.

Your local librarian can also be a great teacher, even if the library has no special collections that are of interest to you. Find out when the librarian has a little time to discuss your collection with you. Once he or she knows your interests, the librarian can steer you to reference books and new acquisitions in your field. It's a good idea to make the local library a regular stop in your weekly round of activities.

REFERENCE BOOKS

Reference books are the map to the hidden treasure. They will add scope and dimension to your collection or collecting areas by leading you to other books and enlarging your knowledge of your field and subjects related to it. And they will provide the provenance of many, if not all, of the books in your collection. A good collection has a good reference library contained within it. A great collection has a great reference library.

Reference books may be more expensive than other books, because often they are costly to produce and take a long time to come into being. They may be printed in a limited edition. But they are worth their weight in gold. The knowledge, provenance, and help in cataloguing you gain will more than pay for the initial investment.

What is a reference book? Any book that you buy primarily not to read but to use as a source of information. Dictionaries and encyclopedias are reference books. *Subject Collections*, which I mentioned earlier in this chapter, is a reference book.

Then there are the reference works written for a particular subject or area. For example, in Chapter 3 I mention a reference work on the fine arts, E. Louise Lucas's *Art Books: A Basic Bibliography on the Fine Arts*. The word "bibliography" is the clue. This book consists of a listing of titles dealing with the fine arts. There are many similar reference works in nearly every subject, hundreds of books listing titles printed since Gutenberg—even before, in the case of illuminated manuscripts. These reference works fall into the category listed in dealers' catalogues as "books about books." That is really what they are all about.

Other reference books are more concerned with a subject in general than with the books about it, but they mention books as well. For example, in *Theory and Design in the First Machine Age*, Reyner Banham includes in his discussion descriptions of books that are important to some modern art movements.

Ask the reference librarian at your library to show you the reference works in the area that you are interested in. But don't be restricted to them. Most of us think of reference works in too narrow a framework. Any work that adds background or insight to an area that you are interested in, and any work that has a good bibliography that leads you to other works in the field, can be considered a reference work.

My suggestion to you is to take note of the titles of reference books as you come across them. You can note them on 3 × 5 cards, perhaps a different color card from the ones you use for cataloguing. Later you can check the volume at the library—or at the bookstore, if it is still in print. If the reference work can add to your knowledge or your collection, if it lists books that you have or want, then it is important for you. If you feel that you would like to refer to it again and again, then it should be in your own library.

KEEPING UP WITH THE LITERATURE

Within a short time you will have an idea of what figures, movements, places, objects, or events fall within your collecting areas. At first you may have to seek them out, but soon you will be able to identify more and more of them; and as you read your local newspaper you will begin to turn to the book review section first to see if anything new has been published in your collecting area. New publications are also announced in book journals (see Chapter 3), specialized subject journals, and trade and professional journals (see Chapter 7).

Remember that the elements of your collecting consist of the present as well as the past. Modern scholarly research in every field is published constantly, and it can add new insights and depth to your knowledge and your collection. Buying a book that is available now will save you expense and work later on, when the title is out of print.

Keeping up with the literature in your field is essential. A library that isn't growing is a library that is stagnating. Collection development, whether in an institution or at home, is an active undertaking. You may not always have the money to buy good items for your collection, but you should always have your collection in mind and take note of publications as they appear.

YOU BE THE JUDGE

You now have the know-how to build and shape your own collection. You can appreciate what other collectors have done—for the methodology is always similar—but the trip you are taking must be your own. Don't be a mere follower of what other people have collected. Don't be ashamed to say that a book or a field of collecting isn't of interest to you, if it isn't. You don't have to like all books. This doesn't imply the books you don't like are bad; it is simply that they do not fit your interests at the present time. Stick to your guns, and don't be bullied. Once you feel confident enough to stand up for your own likes and dislikes, you are on the way to building a collection that is truly unique and individual. Be patient; it may take a little time before you can feel this commitment, but take my word, the day will come.

Collecting is a journey along the paths of your own interests. (And promise me that you will enjoy the trip.) But inherent in every journey's end is the beginning of the next one, just as every artist's finished work contains the seeds of the one he or she has yet to begin. The dynamics of collecting are the same as the dynamics of living; our fortunes change—our values change. The collection should undergo a similar metamorphosis.

A TIME FOR PRUNING

As you grow and change, so will your collection. Some books will no longer have the same meaning as they did when you first began collecting them. Scan your bookshelves. Remove a book. Look at it—open it up, let it speak to you. Is there a bond? Is there something between you and the volume in your hand? If so, then return the volume to its place on the shelf. If not, remove it and put it on a shelf with other books that seem to be unresponsive. This is what I call the limbo shelf, the shelf of uncertainty. The books somehow don't fit in with the others. They do not evoke a response in you; they are dead. You are not sure if you want to give them up or keep them. It's like the old clothes hanging in your closet. You can't dispose of them, because they were once a part of you. They still hold some kind of attraction, but not enough for you to wear them. So they remain in limbo.

My suggestion is to leave the books in limbo for awhile. Then go back to them again. If they still don't speak to you, or if you feel strongly that they aren't part of the *now* you, then it is time to dispose of them.

A friend of mine used to say, "I may not know what I want, but I certainly know what I don't want." For many of us, it's not that easy. It implies making a decision and committing oneself to it. It means separating the wheat from the chaff, unless you have purchased the volume for investment reasons—in which case you will not be in this predicament. It's easier if you remember that there is no moral judgment involved in this decision, only a personal one.

I've had this problem myself. The first collection I sold was my own library. But most booksellers are unconscious collectors, and I vowed I would get those books again—and I did, several times over. The difference between the bookseller and the collector is that the bookseller is selling for profit, while the collector is disposing of what no longer fits into the collection. If you wait and see how permanent your feelings are before you rid yourself of that part of the collection which is no longer meaningful, you will not regret the decision to part with these books. Give yourself enough time to convince yourself that the feelings are not passing, and that these books are no longer important to you.

Then dispose of the books at your leisure. They have been there for awhile already, so why rush? Don't fret. When the opportunity comes, you will sell them, trade them, or donate them, as you see fit.

I'll tell you how in Chapter 10.

Parting Is Such Sweet Sorrow . . .

Especially when there are so many memories, triumphs, discoveries, good buys, cunning swaps. Yes, it is always hard to part with a book that you once loved. You may have cut your teeth on those volumes, you may have a sentimental attachment to them—but, alas, they are no longer vital, no longer give you the excitement or stimulation that they used to. Perhaps you are now collecting other books, and the collection is growing more personal; the orchestral works have given way to chamber music, and you want to hear each individual voice. Or perhaps you feel that this is the right time to dispose of your investment; perhaps prices for these books are at an all-time high, and you would like to put your money into costlier books now, or try another venture altogether. Or perhaps you are moving and you wish to take with you only those volumes that are most meaningful to you. Or you are retiring and you don't have the need for books about the profession that you have just left.

There are dozens of reasons for selling part or all of a collection; I have listed just a few of them. You don't really need any reasons other than a feeling that you don't want to own these books any longer. Period.

My hope is that when you dispose of these books, you will buy others in their place. I hope that your collection continues to grow, and that you continue to grow, and that you collect books that reflect how you feel and see your world now. Not books just because they were given to you; not books you bought just because they were on sale. From now on, selectivity should be your goal, and the books you select should be those that really turn you on.

SETTING A PRICE ON YOUR BOOKS

Where do you go from here? There are several roads open to you. You should have little trouble in disposing of your books. But first you must set a price on them.

Make sure the books you wish to sell have been catalogued. They should have been catalogued before you decided to sell them, and you should have a record of the price you paid, including all the incidental costs associated with the purchase—the cost of the bank draft, postage, insurance, repairs, etc. This information gives you a base figure. The year of the purchase should also have been noted on the card. Say you bought the book five years ago for $25. It was out of print then; it is more in demand now; what would be a fair market price? Well, considering all the work involved, the cataloguing, insurance, upkeep, or overhead, you should be able to add on at least 12 percent a year to your original purchase price. This figure is just an estimate, but if you received $40 for a book you bought five years ago for $25, at least you wouldn't be losing anything.

The back of the catalogue card should also have records of the prices the title has reached in recent auctions, in dealers' catalogues, and in specialist bookstores. If you have kept up with the prices other people in the field consider fair, you will know just how high or low you want to go. The final judgment is yours. You must feel good about the sale. You must not be too greedy or, on the other hand, too gracious, unless you want to give the book away at a price lower than its fair market value.

It is extremely important to have all the pertinent facts about the book's provenance listed on the card, too—the edition, dedications, bindings, bibliographic citations, and so on; and its condition. Remember, these factors can enhance or detract from the book's value.

APPRAISALS

If you want to sell your entire collection en bloc and you haven't done the groundwork to know what the collection is worth, you may consider a professional appraisal. Before you consider taking this action, though, let me say that if the collection is worth less than $1,500, it doesn't pay to have it appraised. The cost is too high to make it worthwhile.

Other reasons for a professional appraisal are that your insurance company requires it, or that if you are donating the collection to an institution, or have inherited it, the IRS requires an appraisal for tax purposes; the IRS is reluctant to accept a donor's or heir's own evaluation, except on amounts under $200.

If you must have your collection appraised, call in an expert in the field, either a bookseller, a professional appraiser, or an auction house. Booksellers are the natural choice, since they know the field intimately and can give you an up-to-date evaluation. The bookseller you select should be an expert in the field of your collection. Thus, he or she will have had the experience of dealing with the books and materials for many years, will have issued lists or catalogues, will have attended auctions, and will have the reference library to provide the provenance for your collection. In other words, he or she is a recognized authority in your areas of collecting.

Or you may use a professional appraiser, a person whose major source of livelihood is doing appraisals. Professional appraisers may be members of professional organizations such as the American Society of Appraisers, but not necessarily; many professional appraisers are also librarians or work for auction houses. The professional appraiser should be as familiar with your field as booksellers are, and have at his or her command the knowledge, experience, and resources to arrive at the fair market value.

Auction houses are another source of appraisals. The larger auction houses charge from 1 to 1½ percent of the collection's value for an appraisal, and will provide a written evaluation. If you sell the collection at auction in the same house that appraised it within a year from the date of the appraisal, most houses deduct the appraisal fee.

A bookseller or professional appraiser will charge you either a percentage of the total worth of the collection or a fixed fee on a per diem basis. The per diem basis is best, because it eliminates any unconscious tendency to price the items a little higher than the fair market value. Per diem rates vary with the area of the country and the reputation, expertise, and *chutzpah* of the dealer, from about $180 to $400 per day. If the collection is small it can usually be appraised in one day, but most take two or three days, including the written appraisal.

Always insist on a written appraisal. If the appraiser doesn't want to give you one, forget about him or her. No insurance company, internal revenue agent, or librarian will accept a verbal evaluation. It must be in writing. It should contain a listing of all the books and a price for each volume or set. The appraisal should also include a visit to your home or office so that the appraiser can actually see the books, inspect them carefully, and then evaluate them. The individual nature and condition of the books must be seen to be evaluated.

Whoever appraises the collection is responsible for proving the evaluation if the IRS decides to question it. And believe me when I say they do, especially with larger collections that are given to libraries as a tax deduction. The government is very strict. More than one-half of the appraisals I do are checked later by an agent in my office. For this reason, I always include a half day more in the cost of the appraisal, because it's been my experience that it takes that long for me to support and prove my prices; and my appraisals have never been disallowed.

If you are paying the appraiser per diem, the better your records and catalogue cards, the less the appraisal will cost you in time and money. The appraiser has all the facts right there on the cards. All you have to do is photocopy the cards and give the appraiser a set to keep for his or her records; remember, the original cards must never leave your premises.

WHO WILL BUY MY BOOKS?

When you are selling your books, you should consider all types of potential buyers: private collectors in your field—if you do not have a list of their names, you can refer to the *International Directory of Book Collectors*; booksellers, who are listed, with their specialities, in the ABAA's membership list, the *International Directory of Antiquarian Booksellers*, and the *AB Bookman's Yearbook*; and libraries with collections in your field — listed in Ash and Lorenz's *Subject Collections*.

Don't hesitate to send a list of the books you have for sale to foreign dealers if the titles are expensive or the list is extensive enough to warrant the outlay of airmail postage. Their addresses and specialities are also listed in the *International Directory of Antiquarian Booksellers*.

SELLING PROCEDURES

You know, this venture into the marketplace makes you, in effect, a bookseller—for the time being, at least. It's a good thing, too. Now you can appreciate the dealer's efforts. You will be a more sympathetic buyer in the future. At least you will lose the prejudices you may have had about the book trade and its pricing. I always encourage collectors to go into the marketplace and prove themselves in battle. It adds a new dimension to the

collecting experience. It is really a lot of fun, too. And now that
the tables have turned and you and I are indeed brothers in books,
I will give you some tips on how to sell your books in a professional
manner.

Prepare a list. The first step is to make a list of the books you
have for sale. If your catalogue cards contain all the pertinent
information, all you have to do is tape the cards in alphabetical
order to sheets of paper, type your name and address on the top
of each sheet, and have the sheets photocopied. If the cards are
not neatly typed, you'll have to have the sheets typed now. Give
the typist photocopies to type from, or have them typed on your
premises—which, as I hope you remember, the cards never leave.

Before you photocopy plenty of copies of the resulting list,
enough to send to all the collectors, dealers, and libraries you
have selected as being suitable, you must decide whether to mark
in the prices for each book on the list.

Include your prices. There are two schools of thought concerning
pricing. One believes that you shouldn't indicate a price for each
title; just list the titles and state in a cover letter that you are
interested in selling the volumes, and that if the recipient is
interested, he or she should make an offer for the lot or for
individual titles. The other school of thought, which I personally
agree with, says to state a price for each title and in the cover
letter say that you will consider all offers for individual titles or
for the entire collection. The latter approach is more professional,
knowledgeable, and clear-cut. It shows that you are aware of what
is going on in the marketplace and that you are asking for a fair
market value. Dealers, librarians, and private collectors will see
that they are dealing with a sophisticated collector and they will
respect the prices, if they are fair prices.

If you don't list prices, you will receive bids that are laughably
low. If you do list prices, the bids will be within a reasonable
range of the listed price. That's only fair. You are in the market

to make as much as you can, and your experience, work, and effort should be rewarded.

Write a cover letter. After you have listed the books, you should prepare an introduction to it that lists the conditions of sale. The introduction can go right on the list, if the list is short—say one or two pages. Usually, however, it is better to prepare and photocopy a separate cover letter. Make certain, however, that your name and address are given on each page of the list, in case the list and the letter get separated.

Here is a sample cover letter:

Name

Date

Dear Bookperson:

After considerable thought, I have decided to sell part of my collection of ———— books, which I have been collecting for the last ———— years. The direction of my collection has changed, and I no longer need the books on the enclosed list. I am offering them to you, subject to prior sale, cash with order [or, if you wish, the terms can be arranged according to the way the books are sold; if they are sold for less than the listed price, cash is usually asked for, to compensate for the reduction in the selling price], payment within thirty days. Postage and registration or insurance are extra.

I will consider selling the collection en bloc, or individual titles. I am open to reasonable offers as well.

This list is being sent to others, so please let me know whether you are interested as soon as possible.

Sincerely yours,

Signature

Enc.

If you would be willing to trade your books (see p. 90), add this paragraph before the closing:

I am also including my want list and would consider trading the titles listed for the titles searched for.

This letter is flexible, and it should get replies. Send it out, and see what happens.

Advertise your list. Now that your list is ready, why not advertise it? Place a small ad in the books for sale section of the *AB*:

Now ready: List of ————— [number] books on ————— [subjects]. Send SASE & $1 [if you decide to charge for postage] to ————— [name], ————— [address].

If the list is heavier than one ounce, you should charge for postage. Remember, first-class is now 15¢ for the first ounce and 13¢ for each additional ounce up to twelve ounces. You can send the list by third-class mail, which is cheaper; but it's also slower.

Sold to the highest bidder. You have solicited bids on your entire collection, so naturally you will want to wait for the highest bidder. The first rule for getting top dollar for your books is never to sell in haste, if you can possibly avoid it. If you have prepared the entries with a complete description and have followed all the other steps I suggested, all your work and expense will be amply compensated in due time.

There is a negative psychological factor at work in hasty sales. Somehow the potential buyer can detect a sense of urgency and will take advantage of it by coming in really low. Never make it known that you need cash right away, because the opposite side will usually try to clobber you. I hope that you never get into a position where you are so desperate financially that you must sell in haste. In all transactions, whether buying or selling, a calm, confident, firm approach and a take-it-or-leave-it attitude work best. You will be respected, even if the sale isn't consummated. I have learned over twenty-five years of buying and selling that the impressions you make at the start will set the tone and

132   *Parting Is Such Sweet Sorrow . . .*

manner for all future transactions. So start right. Act the way you would if you were buying.

Wait at least three weeks to see what kinds of bids you receive for the entire collection. You will find that libraries and dealers are slower in responding to you than private collectors. Libraries have to check their holdings; college and university libraries have to see if faculty or bibliographers need the books. Dealers have to check their customers' want lists as well as their own desiderata; sometimes, if the titles fall outside their specialty areas, they may offer them to customers and only buy them if the customer wants them.

While you are waiting, you can note the offers you receive for the individual titles as well as the whole collection. (The common practice is to extend at least a 10 percent discount on the marked prices if the collection is sold as a whole.) It is courteous to respond to offers to buy individual books. Be honest; state in your reply that you are waiting until such-and-such a date before making a decision on whether to sell the books individually or en bloc, but that you will let them know the final outcome whether you accept their offer or not. This is especially important for institutions, which may have set aside funds against the purchase and want to release the money for other purposes if they are unsuccessful. You can photocopy a reply on the back of a postcard:

Thank you for your offer to buy item(s) ———. I am waiting until ——— [date] before making a decision as to selling the entire collection or individual titles. If you do not hear from me, then, the item(s) or collection has been sold.

Sincerely yours,
Name

First come, first served. Be fair. If you get two equally high bids for the whole list, the bid you receive first should be the one to get the collection. If you sell the titles individually, the rule is still first come, first served.

Sending the books. Send the books to your successful customers promptly. Pack them carefully in an air bag or a carton, and send them by book rate, insured for the value of the selling price, or by United Parcel Service, insured—whichever is cheaper and more convenient (United Parcel Service is cheaper for heavier packages). Postage and insurance are always charged to the customer.

If you are sending books overseas, get a free copy of Publication 51, *International Postage Rates and Fees*, from your post office. If the parcel weighs eleven pounds or less, it can go by book rate. Book rate parcels must have one side left unsealed, but you can tie it with string. They cannot be insured, but they can be registered. Over eleven pounds, they go by parcel post and can be insured, for most countries.

Billing. If you don't know your customer, it is wise to send an invoice requesting payment before you send the books. This type of invoice is called a "pro forma." If you do know the customer, you can send an invoice with the books and mark it payable in thirty days, or sixty days, or whatever. Always send at least two copies of your invoice, one to be returned with the check or payment. You can buy commercial invoice forms in your stationery store and have a rubber stamp made with your name, address, zip, and telephone number to personalize them.

It's not all for you. The difference between what the books cost you plus all the expenses of preparing and mailing the list (typing, photocopying, postage, etc.) and packing the books, and what you sold the books for is taxable income and should be reported on your income tax. If by chance you take a loss—and I hope that will never be the case—you should report the loss; it's deductible.

SELLING AT AUCTION

If you do not receive the response you expected from your list— and I doubt that this will happen—and if the collection is worth over $1,000, it may pay to put the books up for auction. I use this figure because most of the larger auction houses won't take a collection that they feel will not bring at least $1,000, and a few now have $2,000 limits. Under these amounts, it simply doesn't pay for them to catalogue the collection, print the catalogue, conduct the auction, bill the customers, and pay you.

There are a few things to keep in mind about auctions. One is that the auction house will take a commission on the items sold. The commission varies from house to house. Inquire what the commission is before committing the books. Auction houses also charge for insurance to cover the books while they are in their possession, and photographs, if needed for the catalogue.

There is also a wait in the larger auction houses before they can incorporate your collection and catalogue it. If your cataloguing is good, it will facilitate matters considerably, but still the auction house's catalogue has to be printed and mailed. You will also have to wait from thirty to sixty days for payment after the books have been sold. In all, the procedure can take from six to nine months.

If you do consign the books, to avoid getting clobbered be sure to attend the auction so that you can bid up the prices of your own books. If the auction house looks down on this practice—and most don't; in fact, they like it, because it means a higher price and a bigger commisison for them—then have a friend or relative bid. Pick an experienced person, though. They must know just when to leave the bidding; otherwise they will end up owning your books and you will have to buy them back at the price they were knocked down for.

Also be sure that you set reserves on the individual items or lots, if the auction house allows you to. A reserve is a price below which the items will not be sold. If the books don't reach the reserve, they are returned to you, and you pay 5 percent for the buy-back privilege. It is much better to buy back good books at 5 percent of the reserve, however, than to see them go for a low price.

TRADING

You may receive a reply from the list stating that the person has a book on your want list and would like to trade it for one on your sales list. You're lucky; it's a great opportunity to dispose of an item you don't want and get one you do want. The trade can be concluded if you feel that each book is worth about the same. Therefore, you should know the fair market value of the books you are searching for. If you don't, and you receive the offer to exchange, you can always reply that you will let the person know in a couple of weeks. In the meantime, you can research the offered title. If you find that the offered book is worth less than the one you have for sale, you can ask for another book as well—if the person has offered you more than one title—or you can suggest that you are interested in the volume offered but want some cash as well. The amount of cash you ask for should be the difference between the worth of the two books.

EXCHANGE ACCOUNTS

Exchanging is similar to trading except that the swap is neither for cash nor for a specific volume. Rather, the buyer sets up a credit for the seller. For example, libraries like to sell their duplicates on an exchange account. I buy their duplicates for x amount of dollars and give them in return a credit on exchange account. That means the library has x amount of dollars with which to order books from our catalogues; or we will order new books for them from the publisher, or act as their agent in auction, or whatever they wish, almost, for the amount that they have credit for over the fiscal year. Libraries might be more hesitant to make this sort of arrangement with private collectors, who aren't in a position to supply the volume of books needed. But perhaps a dealer will be interested in buying your books and offering you an amount on an exchange account in return, which you can absorb in purchases.

If a dealer offers you an exchange account, before you accept make sure you know the dealer well. It is best if the dealer is a specialist in your areas or carries enough of your type of books; then the credit will be absorbed easily within the period you specify.

DONATIONS

Instead of selling your books, you may wish to give them to your alma mater or to a library that has a good collection of material similar to yours and has been helpful in getting you started. Institutions count on receiving donations from friends and neighbors, former pupils, and even from business firms. The Harvard and Yale libraries are great because many of their collections come from former students, faculty, and staff. These libraries are in there early, laying the field for future donations when the donors are still undergraduates using the libraries as part of their required course work. Other libraries do the same, but on a smaller scale.

Supporting the library that helped provide you with an education or that helped you start your collection is a small way of repaying it, and it is a very satisfying and lasting way of being remembered. You also have the satisfaction of knowing that the books you donate will be cared for in a professional manner.

Gifts to libraries are considered charitable donations, and as such are tax deductible. If the value of your donation is over $200, you will probably have to have the books appraised (see p. 126) if you wish to take the deduction. The library probably won't appraise them, because the IRS prefers appraisals by persons not associated with the donor or donee. The appraiser should send you a written appraisal, one copy of which you submit to the library. For more information about this sort of thing, see IRS Publication 561, *Valuation of Donated Property*; and also consult your lawyer and your accountant, because various charitable organizations have different statuses according to IRS.

LEAVING IT ALL BEHIND

If you plan to donate books after you are no longer here, or if you want your executor or heirs to sell your collection, have your lawyer write all the details into your will. If you are leaving the books to a library, say so, and say which library; if special provisions are to be made for housing the collection, these facts should be included. If you want your collection sold at auction, state whether it is to go to a particular auction house, or to the one with the minimum commission. If the books are to be sold to a dealer, mention which dealers you want to be contacted.

Leave nothing to chance or interpretation. State that all the expenses—appraisal, commissions, cataloguing, photos, moving, executor's fee—are to be deductible from the estate as necessary expenses. The more specific you are with these so-called minor details, the less headaches and delays for your heirs.

In these ways, you can enjoy the collection now and provide for its enjoyment by others later.

Afterword

I never expected to be a bookseller; like most of us, I got into my job quite by chance. It was the summer of 1953. I had been working as a sculptor's assistant in Springfield, Massachusetts, helping Ibram Lassaw do the sculpture for a synagogue. I returned to New York to look for a part-time job that would help see me through my next semester at NYU. In *The New York Times*, I spotted an ad for a part-time packer who could read French and German—somewhat unusual requirements for a packer, but I qualified, so I applied for the job.

That's how I met Paul Gottschalk. He was seventy-three at the time, a small, white-haired man who had been a noted bookseller in Berlin and had escaped to The Hague when the Nazis came into power. When the Germans invaded Holland in 1939, Mr. Gottschalk was, fortunately, visiting the United States. He remained here, starting his business all over again—from a hotel room, at first; his stock had been left behind in Holland.

Mr. Gottschalk—P.G., I called him—paid me 75¢ an hour to begin with. For that I organized his storeroom for him—until then, it had been a labyrinth of unpacked crates filled with the academic and scientific periodicals he specialized in—and packed the outgoing orders. And I listened and learned, for P.G. was at heart a pedagogue, with a need to teach all the bright, young, loyal workers whom he had the knack of finding. P.G. and I and later Bob Nikirk, now the librarian of the Grolier Club, would work Saturdays and listen to P.G. talk about the book trade in Europe before both world wars. Once a month he quizzed us to see if we really understood what we were doing, and he would scold us or box our ears if we answered stupidly. "A grown-up must do it!" he'd say if we called on him for help.

It was P.G. who encouraged me to become a bookseller in the fields I loved and knew so well—the arts, architecture, modern illustrated books. I worked for him, in positions of increasing responsibility, until 1957. Then I established my own business.

I've never regretted it. Antiquarian bookselling is one of the last professions where you can run your own business just the way you see fit—a last stronghold of individualistic capitalism, a libertarian's goal, an anarchist's dream. You can arrange the business to suit your own personality, your own interests, and your own clientele. It can be carried out in a home, an office, a shop, a loft—wherever you like. You can work as many or as few hours as you want to. You set your own prices; yet no one dealer can monopolize the trade, for there are too many dealers, and too many books. Professionalism is high, and competition is keen—and healthy, because it keeps us on our toes.

The book business is flexible enough to change as its practitioner changes. Like good wine, it ages beautifully. And as for you, the older you get, the better you get. Very few dealers ever retire. They may slow down some, but they find it hard to quit altogether.

I've been lucky. My job includes two loves of mine: books and the arts. I was able to hook my gig to the stars, and so I am a happy man.

I have met many fine people—private collectors, librarians, and colleagues—who have helped me by acquainting me with subjects, areas, and items that I was previously unaware of. One of the "bennies" of all this activity is that one is able to give something back—service, experience, knowledge. I hope this book has given some of that to you.

Appendix

A Compendium of Collectors' Associations, Professional Associations, Auction Houses, and Book Museums, Special Libraries, and Exhibition Centers

Collectors' Associations

Bibliographical Society of America. P.O. Box 397, Grand Central Station, New York, New York 10017.
Book Club of California. 545 Sutter Street, San Francisco, California 94102.
Caxton Club. 2223 South Parkway, Chicago, Illinois 60649.
The Club of Odd Volumes. 77 Mount Vernon Street, Boston, Massachusetts 02108.
Grolier Club. 47 East 60 Street, New York, New York 10022.
Private Libraries Association. 3B Hurlingham Court, Ranelagh Gardens, London SW6 3UN, England. American Membership Secretary, Box 6, Nevada City, California 95959.
The Rosenbach Foundation. 2010 DeLancey Place, Philadelphia, Pennsylvania 19103.
Rowfant Club. 3028 Prospect Avenue, Cleveland, Ohio 44115.
Zamorano Club. c/o Mr. Tyrus G. Harmsen, Occidental College, Los Angeles, California 90041.

Professional Associations

American Institute of Graphic Arts. 1059 Third Avenue, New York, New York 10021.

American Library Association. 50 East Huron Street, Chicago, Illinois 60611.

American Society of Appraisers. Dulles International Airport, Box 17265, Washington, D.C. 20041.

Antiquarian Booksellers' Association (ABA). 154 Buckingham Palace Road, London SW1W 9TZ, England.

Antiquarian Booksellers' Association of America, Inc. (ABAA). 50 Rockefeller Plaza, New York, New York 10020.

Antiquarian Booksellers' Association of Japan (ABAJ). 29, San-ei-cho, Shinjuku-ku, Tokyo 160, Japan.

Appraisers Association of America. 541 Lexington Avenue, New York, New York 10022.

Associação Brasileira de Livreiros Antiquarios. Rua Cosme Vlho 800, Rio de Janeiro, Brazil.

Associazione Librai Antiquari d'Italia. Via Jacopo Nardi 6, 50132 Florence, Italy.

Den Danske Antikvarboghandlerforening. Kron-Prinsens-Gade 3, DK-1114 Copenhagen K, Denmark.

Finska Antikvariatforeningen. Norra Magasinsgatan 6, Helsinki 13, Finland.

Middle Atlantic Chapter (MAC) of the ABAA. 50 Rockefeller Plaza, New York, New York 10020.

Nederlandsche Vareenigung van Antiquaren. Delilaan 5, Hilversum 1304, the Netherlands.

Norsk Antikvarbokhandlerforening. Ullevålsveien 1, N-1001, Oslo, Norway.

Svenska Antikvariatföreningen, Birger Jarlsgatan 32, 11429, Stockholm, Sweden.

Syndicat Belge de la Librarie Ancienne et Moderne. 112, Rue de Trèves, Brussels 1040, Belgium.

Syndicat de la Librarie Ancienne et du Commerce de l'Estampe en Suisse, Trittligasse 19, CH-8001, Zurich, Switzerland.

Syndicat de la Librairie Ancienne et Moderne (SLAM). 117 Boulevard Saint-Germain, 75006, Paris, France.

Verband der Antiquare Österrichs. Grünangergasse 4, A-1010 Vienna I, Austria.

Verband Deutscher Antiquare, e. V., Leonhardsplatz 28, D-7000, Stuttgart 1, Germany.

Auction Houses

Americana Mail Auction. 4015 Kilmer Avenue, Allentown, Pennsylvania 18104.

Astor Galleries. 754 Broadway, New York, New York 10003.

Bonhams Montpelier Galleries. Montpelier Street, Knightsbridge, London SW7 1HH.

California Book Auction Galleries. 270 McAllister Street, San Francisco, California 94102.

Christie, Manson & Woods International, Inc. 502 Park Avenue, New York, New York 10022.

William Doyle Galleries, Inc. 175 East 87 Street, New York, New York 10028.

Samuel T. Freeman & Co. 1808-10 Chestnut Street, Philadelphia Pennsylvania 19103.

Harris Auction Galleries. 873 North Howard Street, Baltimore, Maryland 21201.

Lubin Galleries. 72 East 13 Street, New York, New York 10003.

Montreal Book Auctions, Ltd. 1529 Sherbrooke Street West, Montreal H3G 1L7 Quebec, Canada.

Northwest Book Auction. 3 Blodgett, Clarendon Hills, Illinois 60514.

Phillips. 525 East 72 Street, New York, New York 10021.

Plandome Book Auctions. P.O. Box 395, Glen Head, New York 11545.

Sotheby Parke Bernet. 980 Madison Avenue, New York, New York 10021; 34 & 35 New Bond Street, London W1A 2AA, England.

Swann Galleries, Inc. 104 East 25 Street, New York, New York 10010.

Book Museums, Special Libraries, and Exhibition Centers

Antiquarian Booksellers Center. 50 Rockefeller Center, New York, New York 10020.

Center for Book Arts. 15 Bleecker Street. New York, New York 10012.

Huntington Library & Art Gallery. 1151 Oxford Road, San Marino, California 91108.

Morgan Library. 29 East 36 Street, New York, New York 10016.

National Book League. 7 Albermarle Street, London W1, England.

Newberry Library. 60 West Walton Street, Chicago, Illinois 60610.

Glossary

TERMS AND ABBREVIATIONS COMMONLY USED IN
CATALOGUES

Note: All dimensions given are those used in the American book trade. British and Euopean sizes are more exact, and are usually given in centimeters.

A.E.G.   *See* All edges gilt.

A.L.   *See* Autograph letter.

ALL EDGES GILT (a.e.g.)   The top, fore-edge, and foot of the book are colored gold.

A.L.S.   *See* Autograph letter signed.

ASSOCIATION COPY   A book that has an inscription, usually handwritten, which adds insight, interest, or information about the author, his or her works, or his or her relation to the inscribee. The inscription helps to establish the book's provenance.

AUTOGRAPH LETTER (A.L.)   A handwritten letter.

AUTOGRAPH LETTER SIGNED (A.L.S.)   A handwritten letter signed by the writer.

BACKSTRIP   The covering of the book's spine.

BD.   *See* Bound.

BDS.   *See* Boards.

BLOCK BOOKS   Books produced around the middle of the fifteenth century in Germany and the Netherlands in which the pictures and explanatory text were all printed from woodblocks.

BOARDS (bds.)   Stiff, corrugated, or cardboard material used as covers, either in their natural state or with an outside covering of paper.

BOUND (bd.)   A book with a cover of any type, or a periodical that has a cover other than its published wrappers.

CL.   *See* Cloth.

CLOTH (cl.)   Covers of linen, buckram, or another textile. The cloth is usually pasted over boards.

COLOPHON   An identifying inscription or emblem printed at the beginning or end of the book. The colophon of a limited edition book will state the number of copies printed, the kind of paper used, how many special copies were reserved for the author or artist, and whether the plates were destroyed after the run.

DISBOUND   A book without a cover.

D.J.   *See* Dust jacket.

DUODECIMO (12mo, 12°)   A book approximately 7 to 8 inches tall, between a sextodecimo and octavo in size. To produce the book, sheets of paper are folded so that they each produce twelve leaves (twenty-four numbered pages).

DUST JACKET (d.j.)   A removable cover, usually paper but now sometimes plastic, put over the permanent cover by the publisher.

ED.   *See* Edited, Edition, Editor.

EDGES   The outer surfaces of the leaves of a book.

EDITED (ed.)   Prepared for publication.

EDITION (ed.)   All the copies of a book printed from the same plates or typesetting.

EDITOR (ed.)   A person who gathers material for a book, oversees a text written by others, and/or makes the text more readable.

8VO, 8°   *See* Octavo.

ELEPHANT FOLIO   A book about 23 inches tall.

ENDPAPERS   Sheets of strong paper used to attach the covers to the body of the book. One leaf is pasted to the inside cover, and one leaf is left free.

EPHEMERA   Printed matter originally intended for the wastebasket—manifestos, broadsides, programs, menus, tickets, playbills, etc.—valued for their association with a book, an author, artist, or other celebrity, a movement, or a period of history.

EX.   *See* Example.

EXAMPLE (ex.)   A particular copy of an edition.

EX-LIB.   *See* Ex-library.

EX-LIBRARY (ex-lib.)   Former library copy, with library markings such as labels or blind or ink stamps.

EX LIBRIS   A bookplate printed with the owner's name or initials and usually a design and inscription and attached or tipped in to the inside front cover.

F, F°   *See* Folio.

FOLIO (F, F°, 2°)   The largest size of book, 13 inches tall and up. To make a folio, a whole sheet of paper is folded once, forming two leaves (four numbered pages).

4TO , 4°   *See* Quarto.

FOXED   The pages are discolored with brownish spots.

FREE ENDPAPER   The endpaper that is not attached to the inside front cover.

HALF TITLE PAGE   A page at the beginning of a book containing only the book's main title.

HINGE   The meeting of the spine and the edges of the inner cover behind the line where the pasted endpapers and free endpapers meet.

HORS TEXTE, versos blank (h.t.v.b.) "Hors texte" is French for "outside of the text," and the term usually refers to plates, without printing on the reverse sides. The plates may be tipped in to paper of a different stock from that of the text.

H.T.V.B. *See* Hors texte, versos blank.

I. *See* Index.

ILL., ILLS., ILLUS. *See* Illustrated. Illustration.

ILLUSTRATED (ill., ills., illus.) Containing illustrations.

ILLUSTRATION (ill., ills., illus.) A design, picture, plate, plan, diagram, chart, or map printed within the text.

INCUNABULA Books, pamphlets, calendars, and indulgences printed before 1501.

INDEX (i.) An alphabetical listing of names or topics mentioned in the book, with their page numbers. For serials and journals, the index is usually published after the volume is completed and is usually found in the last issue.

L., LL *See* Leaf.

LEAF (l.; plural, leaves, ll.) A single sheet in a book; each leaf contains two printed pages, one on each side.

LIMITED EDITION An edition limited to a specified number of copies.

N.D. *See* No date.

NO DATE (n.d.) No date of publication mentioned within the book.

NO., NOS., # *See* Number.

NO PLACE (n.p.) No place of publication mentioned in the book.

N.P. *See* No place.

NUMBER (no., #; plural, numbers, nos.) An issue of a periodical.

OCTAVO (8vo, 8°)   A book of about 5 inches wide and 8 inches tall to about 6 × 9 inches. Octavo is the most common size for hardcover books now. To make octavo books, each sheet of paper is folded to make eight leaves (sixteen pages).

// or || These marks, called "parallels," mean "no more published." They are used in connection with serials and periodicals.

PL., PLS.   *See* Plate.

PLATE   An illustration, usually separate from the text. Also, a surface used for printing.

PREF.   *See* Preface.

PREFACE (pref.)   Author's introductory statement.

PRO FORMA INVOICE   An invoice requesting payment before the books are sent.

PROSPECTUS   A publisher's announcement of a forthcoming book, set, or periodical, with information about the price, contributors or authors, date of publication, and binding.

QUARTO (4to, 4°)   A book between octavo and folio in size; approximately 11 to 13 inches tall. To make a quarto, a sheet of paper is folded twice, forming four leaves (eight pages).

REMAINDERS   Slow-selling books that the publishers, and in turn the retailers, sell at a reduced price.

SER.   *See* Series.

SERIES (ser.)   A group of volumes with a common theme issued in succession by a single publisher.

SEXTODECIMO (16mo, 16°)   A small book, approximately 4 inches wide and 6 inches tall. To make it, each sheet of paper is folded four times, forming sixteen leaves (32 pages).

SHAKEN   A book in which the hinges have given way, making the pages loose within the cover.

SIGNATURE   A sheet of paper folded to make one unit of the book. The signatures are gathered and sewn together to form books.

16MO, 16° *See* Sextodecimo.

SLIPCASE A box for a book. The box is enclosed on all sides except the spine.

SPINE The book's backbone, where the signatures are gathered. The spine is covered with the backstrip.

T.E.G. *See* Top edge gilt.

TIPPED IN Fastened lightly to a leaf, the binding, or an inside cover. Usually refers to plates that are pasted onto the page by their upper corners.

TIRAGE French for "a printing." Usually used for a limited edition, often numbered and dated.

TITLE PAGE (t.p.) The title page, near the beginning of the book, lists the title and subtitle of the book, the authors, editors, and/or contributors, the publisher or printer, and sometimes the place and date of publication. The title page information should be used for cataloguing (not the half-title page or covers).

TITLE PAGE INDEX (t.p.i.) Used in describing periodicals, to indicate that the title page and index are present; without a title page and index, the volume is incomplete.

T.L.S. *See* Typewritten letter signed.

TOP EDGE GILT (t.e.g.) Top edge, or head of the leaves of the book, is colored gold.

T.P. *See* Title page.

T.P.I. *See* Title page index.

12MO, 12° *See* Duodecimo.

2° *See* Folio.

TYPEWRITTEN LETTER SIGNED (t.l.s.) A typewritten letter signed by hand.

UNCUT A book with leaves that haven't been trimmed; the edges thus have a natural look. Not the same as unopened.

UNOPENED A book with the sheet folds intact at the top and outer edges. The leaves must be slit open if the book is to be read.

UNPAG. *See* Unpaginated.

UNPAGINATED (unpag.) The pages are not numbered (although each signature may be designated by letter).

WR., WRS. *See* Wrappers.

WRAPPERS (wr., wrs.) Stiff paper covers often used for exhibition catalogues and pamphlets and for some inexpensive popular books published in Europe.

Bibliography

Some Important Trade and Collectors' Journals, Directories, Reference Works, and Books about Collecting

TRADE AND COLLECTORS' JOURNALS

AB Bookman's Weekly. P.O. Box AB, Clifton, New Jersey 07015.

Angebotene und Gesuchte Bücher. Beilage zum Börsenblatt für den Deutschen Buchhandel. Buchhandler-Vereinigung GmbH, 6 Frankfurt am Main 1, Grosser Hirschgraben 17/21, Germany.

Antiquarian Book Monthly Review. 30 Cornmarket Street, Oxford, OXI 3EY, England.

Bibliofile. Box 147, Lewes, Delaware 19958.

Book Collector. 3 Bloomsbury Place, London WC1A 2QA, England.

Book Collector's Market (BCM). P.O.B. 3128, Shiremanstown, Pennsylvania 17011.

Bookdealer. Sardinia House, Sardinia Street, London WC2A 3NW, England.

Book-Mart. P.O. Box 243, Decatur, Indiana 46733.

Book Sales & Wants Advertiser. Hoovey's Ltd., 10 Claremont, Hastings, Sussex, England.

Bulletin du Bibliophile. 18 Rue Dauphine, 75006 Paris, France.

The Clique. 75 World's End Road, Handsworth Wood, Birmingham B20 2NS, England.

Gazzettino Librario. Via J. Nardi, 6. 50132 Florence, Italy.

DIRECTORIES

Adressbuch fur den deutschsprachigen Buchhandel Directory of the German-language book trade). Volume 2, "Booksellers." Buchhandler-Vereinigung GmbH, Adressbuch, Redaktion, Postfach 2404, D-6000 Frankfurt 1, Germany.

Annual Directory of Booksellers in the British Isles Specialising in Antiquarian and Out-of-Print Books. The Clique Ltd., 75 World's End Road, Handsworth Wood, Birmingham B20 2NS, England.

Bookdealers' and Collectors' Year-book and Diary. Sheppard Press, P.O. Box 42, Russell Chambers, Covent Garden, London WC2E 8AX, England.

Bookdealers in North America: A Directory of Dealers in Secondhand and Antiquarian Books in Canada and the United States of America. 7th ed. Sheppard Press, P.O. Box 42, Russell Chambers, Covent Garden, London WC2E 8AX, England.

The International Directory of Antiquarian Booksellers. 6th ed. The International League of Antiquarian Booksellers, 1977. Available from the Antiquarian Booksellers' Association of America, Inc., 50 Rockefeller Plaza, New York, N.Y. 10020.

R. and J. Sheppard, compilers. *The International Directory of Book Collectors, 1978—80.* Trigon Press, 117 Kent House Road, Beckenham, Kent, England.

REFERENCE WORKS

American Book Prices Current (ABPC). New York: Bancroft-Parkman.

Ash, Lee, compiler. *Subject Collections.* 5th ed. New York: R. R. Bowker, 1978.

Books in Print. Authors Index (2 vols.) Subject Guide (2 vols.), Titles (2 vols.). New York: R. R. Bowker.

Hertzberger, Menno, ed. *Dictionary of the Antiquarian Book Trade.* International League of Antiquarian Booksellers. Available through the Antiquarian Booksellers Association of America.

IRS Publication 561. 1977 edition.

McGrath, Daniel, ed. *Bookman's Price Index: A Guide to the Values of Rare and Other Out-of-Print Books*. Detroit: Gale Research Co., published annually.

Mandeville's Used Book Price Guide. 5-year edition, 2 vols. & supplement. Kenmore, Washington: Price Guide Publishers.

Titus, Edna Brown, ed. *Union List of Serials in Libraries of the United States and Canada*. 3rd ed. 5 vols. New York: H. W. Wilson & Co., 1965.

United States Postal Service. *Publication 51, International Postage Rates and Fees*.

Van Allen, Bradley. *The Book Collector's Handbook of Values: 1978–1979 Values*. New York. Putnam's, 3rd ed. rev., 1978.

BOOKS ABOUT COLLECTING

Berkeley, Edmund, Jr., ed. *Autographs and Manuscripts: A Collector's Manual*. New York: Scribner's, 1978.

Booth, Richard. *Book Collecting*. Orlando, Florida: House of Collectibles, 1976.

Carter, John. *ABC for Book Collectors*. Rev. ed. New York: Knopf, 1963.

Carter, John, ed. *New Paths in Book Collecting: Essays by Various Hands*. New York: Arno, facs. of 1934 ed.

Dunbar, Maurice. *Fundamentals of Book Collecting*. Los Altos, California: Hermes, 1976.

Haller, Margaret. *The Book Collector's Fact Book*. New York: Arco, 1976.

Hinds, Marjorie M. *How to Make Money Buying and Selling Old Books*. 10 Maple Street, Laceyville, Pennsylvania 18623: Marjorie M. Hinds.

Kraus, H. P. *A Rare Book Saga: The Autobiography of H. P. Kraus*. New York: Putnam's, 1978.

Lewis, Roy Harley. *Antiquarian Books: An Insider's Account*. New York: Arco, 1978.

Peters, Jean, ed. *Book Collecting: A Modern Guide*. New York: R. R. Bowker.

Rostenberg, Leona, and Stern, Madeleine. *Between Boards: New Thoughts on Old Books*. Montclair, New Jersey: Allanheld & Schram, 1978.

Rostenberg, Leona, and Stern, Madeleine. *Old and Rare: Thirty Years in the Book Business*. Montclair, New Jersey: Allanheld & Schram, 1975.

Slater, J. Herbert. *How to Collect Books*. Reprint of 1905 ed. Chicago: Canterbury Bookshop, 1975.

Sternberg, S. H. *Five Hundred Years of Printing*. 3rd ed. London: Penguin, 1955.

Tannen, Jack. *How to Identify and Collect American First Editions: A Guidebook*. New York: Arco, 1976.

Theberge, C. B. *Canadiana on Your Bookshelf: Collecting Canadian Books*. Don Mills, Ontario: J.M. Dent & Sons, 1976.

Index

ARTHUR H. MINTERS is proprietor and president of Arthur H. Minters, Inc., of New York City, a bookseller specializing in publications on art, architecture, and literature. He was born in New York in 1932 and attended City College of New York, Black Mountain College, New School for Social Research, and received his Bachelor of Arts degree from New York University. He is a contributor to periodicals of interest to bookmen, and has taught a course in book collecting at Marymount Manhattan College. He lives in Manhattan's Greenwich Village with his wife, Frances, and has two daughters, Elizabeth Anne and Michèle Anne.